The PROJECT ACHIEVE Series

STOP and THINK

The Stop & Think SOCIAL SKILLS PROGRAM

Copyright 2001 by Sopris West.
All rights reserved.

07 06 05 04 03   6 5 4 3 2

Edited by Beverly Rokes and Toni Rigby
Text layout and cover design by Sherri Rowe
Cover and spot illustrations by Corbin Hillam

No part of this work may be reproduced or transmitted in any form or by any means, electronic or mechanical, including photocopying or recording, or by any information storage and retrieval system, without the express written permission of the publisher.

ISBN 1-57035-421-9

Printed in the United States of America

Published and Distributed by

Teacher's Manual for PreK–1

Howard M. Knoff, Ph.D.

SOPRIS WEST
EDUCATIONAL SERVICES

4093 Specialty Place • Longmont, CO 80504 • (303) 651-2829
www.sopriswest.com
EDUCATIONAL SERVICES

Copyright 2001 by Sopris West.
All rights reserved.

07 06 05 04 03   6 5 4 3 2

Edited by Beverly Rokes and Terri Eyden
Text layout and cover design by Sherri Rowe
Cover and spot illustrations by Corbin Hillam

No part of this work may be reproduced or transmitted in any form or by any means, electronic or mechanical, including photocopying or recording, or by any information storage and retrieval system, without the express written permission of the publisher.

ISBN 1-57035-421-9

Printed in the United States of America

Published and Distributed by

SOPRIS WEST
EDUCATIONAL SERVICES

4093 Specialty Place • Longmont, CO 80504 • (303) 651-2829
www.**sopriswest**.com

Dedication

To my parents—Max and Terry—who have taught, guided, and supported me through the peaks and valleys of my life's journey and work.

Acknowledgments

There are many people and institutions to thank and to recognize when one completes a major undertaking, such as the publication of this *Stop & Think Social Skills Program Teacher's Manual*. I would like to thank all of the Project ACHIEVE schools and school districts that I have had the privilege of working with over the past ten years—including their students, teachers, support staff, and administrators. Among this group, I would especially like to acknowledge Jesse Keen Elementary School in Lakeland, Florida; Cleveland Elementary School in Tampa, Florida; Hotchkiss Elementary School in Dallas, Texas; Polk County School District in Florida; Hillsborough County School District in Florida; Cleveland Heights/University Heights City School District in Ohio; and the Baltimore City School District in Maryland.

Individuals who deserve special accolades for their work with the Stop & Think process and Project ACHIEVE include Dr. George M. Batsche, the original designer of the Stop & Think process; Lloyd Mattingly, our first Project ACHIEVE coordinator; Drs. Mindy Schuman and Brent Myers, Project ACHIEVE coordinators in the Baltimore City Schools; Michael G. Bailey, the assistant director of Pupil Services for the Cleveland Heights/University Heights City School District; Larry Michaels and Joan Bohmann, Project ACHIEVE coordinators in Anchorage, Alaska; the many graduate students in the School Psychology Program at the University of South Florida; and countless others.

I am also indebted to a number of talented individuals from the Baltimore City Schools who graciously gave their time and creativity to the development of this book. Through their dedication to the Stop & Think process, they have impacted thousands of schoolchildren in Baltimore, and with the publication of this manual, they will now impact hundreds of thousands. These individuals are Kathy Brock, Thersa Clough, Stella Francis, Nicole Green, Kristen Hurdek, Antinetta Hind, Frank Kaufman, Christine King, Lea Klaus, Kate Laetten, Beth Loose, Michele Loving, Amy Martin, Martha Mauretta, Amy Meadows, Melissa Napfel-Sisk, Juan Paz, Deborah Ptak, Elizabeth Renwick, Mollie Sieradzki, Martha Smith, William Tyson, and Victoria Yurek-Gordon.

I thank everyone listed above and all those who aren't listed but who, nonetheless, contributed to the development of the Stop & Think process and/or the content of the *Stop & Think Social Skills Program*.

H.M.K.

About the Author

Howard M. Knoff, Ph.D., is a professor of school psychology at the University of South Florida (Tampa, Florida) and was director of the School Psychology Program there for 12 years. He is also the codirector of the Institute for School Reform, Integrated Services, and Child Mental Health and Educational Policy, and the codirector of Project ACHIEVE, a nationally known school reform project. Dr. Knoff received his Ph.D. from Syracuse University in 1980 and has worked as practitioner, consultant, licensed private psychologist, and university professor since 1978. Known for his research and writing in organizational change and school reform, consultation and intervention processes, social skills and behavior management training, personality assessment, and professional issues, Dr. Knoff has published more than 80 articles and book chapters and delivered over 300 papers and workshops nationally. A recipient of the Lightner Witmer Award from the American Psychological Association's School Psychology Division in 1989 for early career contributions and over $8 million in external grants, he was the 21st president of the National Association of School Psychologists (1989–1990), which now represents over 20,000 school psychologists nationwide.

Relative to his national work in school reform, Dr. Knoff has received at least six outreach federal grants for the U.S. Department of Education Office of Special Education Programs (OSEP) and Office of Educational Research and Innovation (OERI) including a three-year outreach grant for Project ACHIEVE in Baltimore, Cleveland, and Tampa and numerous preservice training grants for training at Jesse Keen Elementary School, Project ACHIEVE's primary training site in Lakeland, Florida. He also was on the writing team that helped produce *Early Warning, Timely Response: A Guide to Safe Schools*, the document commissioned by the President that was sent to every school in the country in the fall of 1998. In addition, Dr. Knoff was invited to discuss Project ACHIEVE at the National Education Goals Panel/National Association of Pupil Personnel Service Organization's "Safe Schools, Safe Communities" meeting in October 1994. He also was a featured speaker at the National Education Association's Safe Schools Summit in Los Angeles (April 1995). And, he was highlighted on an ABC News' *20/20* program entitled "Being Teased, Taunted, and Bullied" on April 28, 1995.

Project ACHIEVE, which is the foundation for the *Stop & Think Social Skills Program*, has been designated a Model Student Services Program in Florida by the State Department of Education in its "Promising Programs and Practices" competitions since 1994; it received an honorable mention in *USA TODAY'S* Community Solutions for Education national awards program for 1995 sponsored by the Coalition on Educational Initiatives; and it was a semifinalist in the 1996 U.S. Department of Education's National Awards Program for Model Professional Development. Project ACHIEVE was highlighted in *Safe, Drug-Free, and Effective Schools for ALL Children: What Works!*, a joint report of the U.S. Department of Education's Safe and Drug-Free Schools and Office of Special Education Programs, April 1998; it was featured at the "Safe and Effective Schools for ALL Children: What Works!" national teleconference, and the Improving America's Schools Conference "Creating Safe Schools and Healthy Students Institute" in September and October of 1999; it was referenced in *Safeguarding Our Children: An Action Guide (Implementing "Early Warning, Timely Response")* published in April 2000; and, finally, Project ACHIEVE has been identified as an effective school reform program by the Center for Effective Collaboration and Practice of the American Institutes for Research, Washington, D.C., since January 1997.

Dr. Knoff has worked with school and parent groups across the country on parenting and discipline issues throughout his career. As a parent of two sons, he knows the importance of both safe and effective schools and socially skilled students. He hopes that some of the "lessons" that he has learned as a parent and professional are helpful to all educators, as well as those concerned with our nation's schools.

Contents

Preface xi

Overview of This Manual 1

Part I

Orientation and Introduction to the Stop & Think Process 3

    Why It Is Important to Teach Students Social Skills 5

    Three Keys to Successful Student Behavior 12

    The Stop & Think Process for Teaching Students Social Skills 18

Part II

Skill Lessons 29

    A Two-Week Schedule for Teaching the Stop & Think Social Skills 31

    The Advanced Preschool to Early Elementary School Social Skills 96

    Other Stop & Think Social Skills 101

    Classroom and Building Routines 104

Part III

Making the Stop & Think Process Work Most Effectively 113

    Talking With Students 115

    Grade-Level and Building-Level Teams 119

    Implementing a Year-Long Social Skills Calendar 123

    Facilitating the Transfer of Training 125

    Evaluating the Stop & Think Implementation Process 130

    Some General Reminders 132

Appendix A: Overview of Project ACHIEVE 135

Appendix B: Essential Readings 149

Appendix C: Glossary 171

Ordering Information 183

Preface

My goal in writing this *Stop & Think Social Skills Program Teacher's Manual* was to provide teachers across the country with an effective, proven way to teach their preschool to early elementary students (PreK–1) the social skills that will help them become more successful socially, academically, and behaviorally. Following the nationally recognized sound principles and procedures of Project ACHIEVE, which is described in detail in Appendix A, the lessons in this manual will guide you, step by step, in:

- Teaching important social skills to your students using simple, effective, age-appropriate procedures that have been successfully implemented in hundreds of school districts across the country.

- Using a consistent "script" as you teach your students each skill and practice the skill with them.

- Demonstrating correctly the social skills that you are teaching, using real-life situations that occur in the classroom and school, and practicing the skills with your students until they can perform them with less and less prompting over time.

- Using the teaching steps and social skills scripts consistently and giving your students incentives to make Good Choices and consequences when they make Bad Choices.

- Helping your students use the skills in different places, with different people, and at different times of the day.

All of the lessons follow the Stop & Think process, in which students are taught to stop and think about how they want to handle a situation before acting, decide whether they want to make a Good Choice or a Bad Choice, think about the steps they need to follow or the Good Choices available to them for carrying out the Good Choice behavior, put their plan into action, and positively reinforce themselves for doing a good job. While teachers of preschool to early elementary school students will spend most of their time *guiding* their students through these steps, these students will use the Stop & Think steps more independently over time, and they will begin to verbalize some specific skills' steps by the end of the first grade.

The interpersonal, problem-solving, and conflict resolution skills you will teach your students using the Stop & Think process start with the listening, following directions, using nice talk, asking for help, waiting for your turn skills, and other skills that your students need to master. As your students continue to learn and use the skills in the *Stop & Think Social Skills Program*, they will be able to make more Good Choices, more agreeably, and, eventually, more independently. Over time, they will become more responsive to adults' Good Choice prompts, demonstrating the prosocial skills that will help them at school, at home, and in the community.

Altogether, there are four *Stop & Think Teachers' Manuals*: this one, written for teachers of PreK to grade 1; one for teachers of grades 2-3; one for teachers of grades 4-5; and one for teachers of grades 6-8. Each focuses on skills that are relevant and needed by students in the targeted age-group. By teaching your students the lessons in the relevant manual, you will provide them with the skills they need to be more successful in school and more prepared for life.

Howard M. Knoff, Ph.D.

Overview of This Manual

This *Stop & Think Social Skills Program Teacher's Manual* is divided into three parts. The first, "Orientation and Introduction to the Stop & Think Process," begins with a discussion of why it is important to teach social skills to young students, and it then introduces the ten social skills considered to be most important for students at the preschool to early elementary school level. The discussion then turns to factors that will be crucial to your teaching success. You'll find that learning the skill steps and the social skills teaching process is important, but just as important are (1) having a strong accountability system in place and (2) teaching with consistency. Indeed, these factors are so important that they are discussed not only in the Introduction but throughout the manual. The Introduction concludes with an explanation of the Stop & Think process used for teaching the social skills and the five important teaching elements:

- Teaching the skills
- Modeling the skills
- Role playing the skills
- Providing performance feedback
- Transferring the training by prompting and having your students use the skills as much as possible during the day

Part II, which makes up the bulk of the manual, begins with an explanation of the two-week schedule and process for teaching the social skills. This is followed by the actual lessons, where you will learn, step by step, how to teach your students the ten core social skills. Skill steps are also provided for ten advanced skills that your students will need as they grow older. The remainder of Part II introduces additional social skills that your students may need, as well as classroom and building routines that, like the social skills, can be effectively taught with the Stop & Think process.

Part III provides suggestions for making the Stop & Think process work most effectively. Topics covered include good ways to talk with your students when using the Stop & Think process; how to teach social skills on a schoolwide basis; how to develop your year-long social skills calendar; how to facilitate the transfer of training across time, settings, people, and situations; and, finally, how to evaluate the process to make sure it is being implemented effectively.

The book concludes with three appendices that contain highly useful information. Appendix A is an overview of Project ACHIEVE, which provides the foundation for the Stop & Think process. Appendix B contains important background information on child development as it relates to teaching social skills as well as on accountability, consistency, and punishment. You are strongly encouraged to read this information. The many suggestions provided will help you improve your efficacy in all aspects of teaching. Finally, Appendix C contains a glossary of important terms.

Also available to aid in your implementation of the *Stop & Think Social Skills Program* is the companion resource, *Stop & Think Reproducible Forms*, which contains cue cards of the ten core and ten advanced social skills covered in this manual, "Stop & Think Stop Signs," a lesson plan form, evaluation forms, and much more.

Part I

Orientation and Introduction to the Stop & Think Process

Why It Is Important to Teach Students Social Skills

The Challenges Facing Students Today

It's hard for students to grow up in today's world. They face pressure at school, at home, with peers, and in the community. They are constantly bombarded with mixed messages about how to behave in different situations.

Clearly, students have important choices or decisions to make almost continuously throughout their day. They also have to respond or react to many interpersonal, problem-solving, and conflict situations. All too often they are angry because they don't get their way, they refuse to follow directions when they are told to do something, their feelings are hurt when peers tease or taunt them, or they don't say no when peers pressure them to engage in inappropriate behaviors or to make harmful decisions.

In today's society, students are more at risk for social, emotional, and behavioral problems than ever before. Indeed, many students today, when compared with students just five years ago, are:

- More angry
- More anxious
- More attention seeking
- More tired and pressured
- Less caring
- More worldly and streetwise
- More impacted by TV, the media, technology (including computer games), and their peer group
- Less responsible
- More defiant and disobedient
- Less impacted by incentives
- More impulsive
- Less impacted by punishment (displaying a "don't care" attitude)
- More interested in immediate gratification

- Less motivated
- Exposed more to sex and drugs
- Less attentive
- Less self-confident
- Lacking self-esteem
- Less self-controlled
- Less concerned with adult approval
- Less able to problem solve on their own

The reasons for these changes typically cluster into the following areas:

- Changes in the nuclear and extended family (e.g., divorce, remarriage)
- Less effective parenting skills at home
- The need for more positive interactions with adults
- Changes in the dynamics of the community and the quality or availability of services
- Decreases in respect, support, caring, and acceptance of others' differences and needs
- The economy and the impact of poverty
- Parents' difficulties in making a comfortable living, and the need to have both parents working to "make ends meet"
- The lack of appropriate role models, good day care opportunities, and adult supervision
- The effect of the media—TV, music, video games, and computers
- The need for improvements in education and the accessibility of positive and long-lasting educational opportunities
- Increased access or exposure to drugs, weapons, and alcohol
- Changes in students—more babies born exposed or addicted to drugs; more students with attention problems and other medical disorders; more students from abusive, dysfunctional, or disrupted families

All of this supports the fact that many students are exposed to difficult situations and challenging life circumstances at very early ages. For those at great risk because of these situations and circumstances, adult supervision and instruction are more important than ever before.

What Teachers Can Do

Given all of this, teachers today often feel that they are constantly monitoring their students, desperately trying to avoid the "Dreaded Ds": Disobedience, Disruption, Defiance, Disrespect, and Disregard. To many teachers, it seems like a never-ending battle, and it often seems like punishment is the only recourse.

For your students to withstand many of the difficult conditions they face, it is critically important that they learn, step by step, the social skills that will help them succeed in the classroom and, ultimately, in life. These interpersonal, problem-solving, and conflict resolution skills are no longer "recommended" skills; in today's world, they are **survival** skills. And we now know that teachers who teach these social skills in their classrooms help their students both behaviorally and academically. Thus, guided by this manual, you will learn to teach the social skills that are most important for students at the preschool to early elementary school ages to be successful.

All of the social skills in this manual are taught following *The Stop & Think Social Skills Program*, a program that has been implemented successfully in hundreds of school districts across the country. The goal of this program and manual is to teach *you* how to teach *your* students how to Stop and Think and make good social and behavioral choices—even when confronted with difficult situations. Specifically, the five steps to the Stop & Think process are discussed, the teaching process is outlined, and lesson plans are provided for teaching the targeted social skills within the Stop & Think context. In addition, a recommended teaching schedule is presented, and numerous examples of role plays, application activities, and reinforcement approaches are provided.

Ultimately, the key to having your students learn social skills is for you to *teach* them how to perform the behaviors that you expect. For this, you will need to do the following:

- Teach each social skill directly using the steps suggested in this manual.

- Use the same "script" to guide your students through each social skill every time you practice.

- Correctly demonstrate the social skill that you are teaching using "real-life" situations that occur in the classroom or school, and then have your students practice the skill until they can do it with less and less prompting.

- Use the Stop & Think steps and the social skills scripts consistently and give your students incentives to make Good Choices and consequences when they make Bad Choices.

- Help your students use the skills in different places, with different people, and at different times of the day.

By doing these things, you will help your students learn to make more Good Choices, more independently, and more automatically.

The Social Skills Covered in This Manual

Although there are hundreds of important social skills for students to learn, this manual focuses on ten core skills considered to be most important for students at the preschool to early elementary school level (preK–1). The skill steps for ten more advanced social skills are also presented, as is a list of additional skills that you might find appropriate for your students. Finally, the skill steps for a number of classroom and building routines are presented that can help your students perform better throughout the classroom and across various school settings.

The ten core skills in this manual were selected because they are so important to the development of good interpersonal, problem-solving, and conflict resolution skills and because they help to create positive classroom climates and safe school buildings. Moreover, they have all been implemented and evaluated by classroom teachers in schools nationwide. These are the skills that your students need to be socially successful with both peers and adults. Finally, they are the skills that are prerequisite to the more advanced skills that your students will need as they grow older.

These ten core social skills at the preschool to early elementary level are:

- Listening
- Following Directions
- Using Nice Talk
- Asking for Help
- Waiting for Your Turn
- How to Interrupt
- Ignoring
- Dealing With Teasing
- Dealing With Losing
- Accepting Consequences

The more advanced social skills at these grade levels and presented later in this manual are:

- Ignoring Distractions
- Rewarding Yourself
- Sharing
- Deciding What to Do
- Asking for Permission
- Joining an Activity
- Using Brave Talk
- Dealing With Being Left Out
- Dealing With Anger
- Apologizing

These 20 (and all other) social skills can be organized into four skill areas: **survival or prerequisite skills**, **interpersonal skills**, **problem-solving skills**, and **conflict resolution skills**. Although some of these skills could be placed into two or more skill areas depending on the situation, this manual uses the following arrangement:

- **Survival or prerequisite skills** are social skills that are used, directly or indirectly, in performing other social skills. Thus, these skills form the foundation for other skills, and, typically, many of them are first taught to students at a young age. The survival skills in this manual are:

    - Listening
    - Following Directions
    - Using Nice Talk
    - Ignoring
    - Ignoring Distractions
    - Rewarding Yourself
    - Using Brave Talk

- **Interpersonal skills** help students to interact appropriately with peers, siblings, older and younger students, parents, teachers, and other adults. In essence, they are the skills that help students to build and maintain social relationships. The interpersonal skills in this manual are:

    - Waiting for Your Turn
    - How to Interrupt
    - Sharing
    - Asking for Permission
    - Joining an Activity

- **Problem-solving skills** help students to solve individual, interactive, or group (e.g., peer or family) problems. Some of these skills prevent problems from occurring, while others help students to respond to a problem so that it does not escalate into a conflict. The problem-solving skills in this manual are:

    - Asking for Help
    - Accepting Consequences
    - Deciding What to Do

- **The conflict resolution skills** help students to deal with significant emotions and emotional situations and to resolve existing intrapersonal and interpersonal conflicts. Among the emotions that students may experience and need to control are anger, embarrassment, frustration, fear, anxiety, jealousy, sadness, impatience, and helplessness. The conflict resolution skills in this manual are:

    - Dealing With Teasing
    - Dealing With Losing
    - Dealing With Being Left Out
    - Dealing With Anger
    - Apologizing

Conclusion

It is important to realize that students will need to be retaught many of the social skills in this manual as they get older. Although the names of the social skills do not change over time, how they are taught and adults' expectations for how students perform these skills *should* change. This is because (1) students, over time, are able to handle increased behavioral expectations due to their development and maturation; (2) students experience or confront more complex and challenging situations as they get older; and (3) adults need to slowly help (i.e., teach) youth to progress behaviorally every day, month, and year, thereby increasing their knowledge and skill level over time.

Thus, your expectations when students perform any of the skills should differ for three-year olds, seven-year olds, and twelve-year olds. As students grow older, they should be expected to perform certain social skills more often, more quickly, for a longer period of time, more independently, and/or with a higher level of self-control. All of this relates directly to the impact of child development and the teaching of social skills. Appendix B highlights a number of developmental characteristics of students at the preschool to early elementary school level. Please read the first part of the Appendix and begin thinking about the ways you currently structure your classroom to maximize the maturation levels of your present students.

Three Keys to Successful Student Behavior

The majority of this manual focuses on how to teach your students the social skills they need to interact appropriately with others, solve problems effectively, and respond to conflict situations successfully. Your success in teaching these social skills initially will depend on how well you learn and teach the skills. However, your success also will be highly dependent on whether you have a strong classroom accountability system in place and whether you teach with consistency. Because of their importance, all three of these factors—skills, accountability, and consistency—are discussed not only here but throughout this manual.

Skills

The first element that is vital to your teaching success is knowledge of the social skills, the skill steps, and the process for teaching them. You will be using this knowledge to help your students master the social skills they need to make Good Choices at school, at home, and in the community. Thus, you will need to be skilled and comfortable with the Stop & Think skills and teaching process, and you will need to teach, model, practice, and reinforce these social skills as much as possible with your students every day.

It is important to understand that your students need to learn these skills to mastery, just as they need to learn academic skills to mastery. That is, they need to be able to successfully or positively demonstrate the skills under all conditions, including conditions of emotionality. You cannot assume that a student has mastered a particular academic or social skill if he or she can perform it when conditions are optimal or calm or when he or she has the time to process through a situation and apply the skill that is required. Instead, you have to make sure—through your use of the Stop & Think teaching process—that your students can perform their social skills automatically and immediately under the most stressful or emotional situations. Only then can you be sure that your students have learned the skills to mastery.

At the same time, you need to be aware that, developmentally, preschool to early elementary school students are socially, emotionally, and behaviorally different from older students. Thus, some levels of emotionality and egocentricity are normal and expected here. The skill "mastery" of these students, then, needs to be put into a realistic context of early childhood development and maturation.

> **Social skills mastery** occurs when students successfully or positively demonstrate an academic skill or interpersonal skill (social skill) under all conditions, including under conditions of emotionality.

Accountability

The second element that is vital to your success in teaching students social skills is accountability. An effective accountability system involves meaningful incentives and consequences to motivate students toward Good Choices and away from Bad Choices, respectively. With the Stop & Think process, students are asked if they are going to make a Good Choice or a Bad Choice, and incentives and consequences are connected to each choice. In a word, a strong accountability system forms the motivational foundation for the Stop & Think process such that students actually perform their social skills. Thus, this system is essential for effective teaching and student behavior.

Expanding briefly, students make Good Choices because they know they will be positively reinforced after making those choices or because they will receive consequences if they make a Bad Choice. Thus, students make Good Choices because they are either motivated toward incentives or motivated away from consequences.

> **Incentives** are actions or responses that occur after or in anticipation of students' Good Choices that motivate their behavior or continuing behavior. Incentives are either extrinsic (e.g., involving tangible or overt reinforcers) or intrinsic (e.g., involving positive self-statements like: "Tell yourself you did a great job!" or "Give yourself a big pat on the back for making such a Good Choice!").
>
> **Consequences** are actions or responses that occur after or in anticipation of students' Bad Choices that motivate them to make a Good Choice the next time. In general, the mildest possible consequence needed to motivate a student's Good Choice should be used. As consequences get more negative or intense, some students need at least the same level of intensity in order for the consequences to maintain their "meaningfulness" over time.

It is extremely important that incentives and consequences be carefully chosen. That is, they must be developmentally appropriate for the age and maturation level of the student, and they should be used only to the degree needed for success. You can identify meaningful incentives by (1) observing what objects, activities, or interactions your students enjoy most; (2) asking your colleagues or your students' parents what the peer group is currently "into"; and/or (3) asking the students themselves what activities or opportunities they enjoy. Many teachers are surprised that preschool through elementary students are motivated most by "small" but more meaningful things, such as time spent together; art and other supplies to be used for creative projects; or books, games, or computer activities that can be educational and fun.

While most students respond positively to such tangible or overt incentives, you should pair these extrinsic reinforcers with social reinforcers (such as a pat on the back) or intrinsic reinforcers (such as positive self-statements like: "Tell yourself you did a Great Job!" or "Give yourself a big pat on the back for making such a Good Choice!"). Over time, this method will help your students become more responsive to the social and intrinsic reinforcers and less dependent on the tangible reinforcers that sometimes get out of control as students expect them more and more. Eventually, the goal is for students to be predominantly intrinsically and self-motivated.

Meaningful consequences are identified in the same way as incentives, but they must be used very carefully. To elaborate:

- Every consequence experienced by a student should be offset by five positive reinforcements or interactions. Both research and practice have shown that students learn and develop best in environments that provide them with five positive interactions for every negative interaction. This is called the 5-to-1 Rule and is discussed in detail in Appendix B.

- Consequences should be as mild as possible in order to motivate a Good Choice. Critically, for some students, as consequences get increasingly negative, they need to be at the same level of intensity as, or more intense than, previous consequences in order for them to maintain their meaning. Unfortunately, this often results in a "death spiral," where you are continually increasing the intensity of certain students' consequences in order to maintain a basic level of behavioral control.

- Consequences are not the same as punishment. Punishment is meant to stop students' inappropriate behavior, while consequences focus on motivating students to use appropriate behaviors in the future. Thus, consequences should, when possible, directly relate to both the Good Choice the student should have made and the Bad Choice the student did make. For example, if a student inappropriately interrupts you, you may have the student wait an extra three minutes for your attention (the consequence related to the student's Bad Choice) and then have the student practice the **How to Interrupt** skill when the three minutes are up (the teaching and reinforcement of the Good Choice behavior).

- Finally, it is important to recognize that consequences may not influence a student's actions immediately. If a student comes from a very inconsistent environment or a traumatic or uneven developmental history, he or she may not believe that you will actually follow through with a stated consequence. Even when you do follow through the first or second time, the student may still be expecting (based on past history) that you will not follow through the next time. Over time, however, as you consistently follow through with appropriate consequences as needed, the student will realize that Bad Choices always result in consequences and that Good Choices are more fun. At that point, the consequences have become meaningful, your behavior has become predictable, and the student will begin to respond with more prosocial behavior and more independent Good Choices.

Significantly, incentives and consequences are influential only *after* a student has learned and mastered specific social skills. Without skills and skill mastery, accountability is meaningless. To demonstrate this, imagine telling a nonswimmer that he can have the $1 million on the other side of a ten-foot-deep pool if he swims to it. While the child may be highly motivated to reach the money, no amount of effort will get him there because he has not mastered the skill of swimming.

You must make sure your students have learned, practiced, and mastered a social skill before using incentives or consequences to motivate its use. If incentives and consequences are applied before skills are mastered, students cannot successfully demonstrate them, and they will react with frustration, anger, withdrawal, resistance, and eventually noncompliance or nonresponsiveness. This very serious emotional and behavioral response is called "learned helplessness"; it can emotionally or behaviorally "paralyze" a child, and it is very difficult to reverse.

However, if incentives and consequences are used *after* social skills are well taught and mastered, then students will respond to them effectively, making primarily Good Choice decisions. You are encouraged to read the additional information about accountability in Appendix B.

Consistency

The third element that is vital to your success in teaching students social skills is consistency. Consistency is important primarily because students want their classrooms and schools to be structured and predictable, and they want to know that the rules and expectations for their behavior will be dependable and fair. Even though they are sometimes resistant, students want to know what the Good Choices and Bad Choices are for specific situations, and they want incentives and consequences to be applied logically and equitably.

Consistency is more of a process than something you teach (such as skills) or provide (such as incentives and consequences). Whether you are teaching social skill steps, modeling a skill, providing practice opportunities, giving performance feedback, reinforcing the skill's use, or providing incentives or consequences, you need to do so in the same way over time, across students, and across situations. While 100% consistency across all students and all situations is impossible to maintain, you need to be consistent at least 80% of the time and reasonably consistent for the other 20%.

Consider what might happen if you do not follow through with incentives and consequences consistently. Say that you have told your students that they will lose time from recess if they do not follow directions, and then you do not *immediately* follow through with the consequence after your students fail to follow directions. Not only might your students lose trust in the incentive and consequence system you are using, but they might also continue to behave inappropriately (at least until you finally enforce the rules with consequences), because they have been allowed to "get away" with the behavior. In addition, they might become angry when you finally *do* enforce the rules, and they might become unmotivated and unresponsive or confused and frustrated because they do not know what is expected of them. Clearly, none of these are desirable outcomes! For more on the relationship of inconsistency to students' Bad Choice behavior, see the readings in Appendix B.

Note that you need to maintain consistency *across* students as well as *within individual* students. As just mentioned, if you are inconsistent with individual students, you may reinforce or strengthen their inappropriate behavior over time, and you may undermine the impact of your accountability system. If you are inconsistent from student to student, then individual students may decide that your classroom incentive and consequence system is confusing (at best) or unfair (at worst). In addition, they may get angry and/or resistant with the system because they feel that (1) you have "favorites" who do not have to comply with the expected behaviors or do not receive the same consequences for inappropriate behavior, or (2) they are being treated differently than others.

Finally, you need to recognize that students have their own "histories of inconsistency" relative to social skills, interventions, and/or accountability. "History of inconsistency" is simply the amount of inconsistency a student has experienced in the past in a certain area. This history will influence how long you need to be consistent when implementing new interventions or programs designed to improve student behavior. Critically, for an intervention to be effective, it must be implemented past the *student's history of inconsistency*.

Let's say, for example, that you were trying to change an inappropriate behavior exhibited by a group of "difficult" students and found that you were introducing a new intervention every three weeks because the students' inappropriate behavior did not change by the end of each three-week cycle. One explanation for the lack of success might be because, over time, these students "learned" that they would get a new intervention and, thus, a new "intervention time clock" if they resisted any intervention for at least three weeks. To break this pattern or history of inconsistency, and to truly evaluate the efficacy of your next intervention, you would have to maintain your next intervention for at least four weeks, optimally for five weeks, and ideally for at least six weeks. By doing this, your students would eventually recognize (1) that their resistance to the intervention was not resulting in a new intervention, (2) that you were consistently maintaining both the behavioral expectations and incentives and consequences inherent in the intervention, and (3) that they were responsible for the outcomes of the intervention (i.e., positive outcomes for Good Choices and negative outcomes for Bad Choices).

Significantly, the impact of inconsistency on students' behavior *can* be reversed. However, the longer a student has experienced inconsistency, the longer you and other adults in that student's life need to maintain a consistent behavioral environment. Remember, however, that 100% consistency is virtually impossible and largely unnecessary. If you are at least 80% consistent over time and 20% reasonably consistent the rest of the time, you will experience the success you desire.

Skills, accountability, and consistency clearly are the keys to your teaching success. While skills must be mastered before incentives and consequences (i.e., accountability) truly become influential, you are encouraged to integrate all three elements and to take them all seriously. As you read the next section of this manual, which discusses the actual process for teaching social skills, bear in mind that how well your students learn and perform these skills will depend, in large part, on your accountability system and consistency.

The Stop & Think Process for Teaching Students Social Skills

Every social skill can be taught with the Stop & Think process, which involves verbalizing and then internalizing the same five steps. These steps are:

1. Stop and Think!
2. Are you going to make a Good Choice or a Bad Choice?
3. What are your Choices or Steps?
4. Do It!
5. Good Job!

The **Stop and Think!** step gives your students the time necessary to calm down and think about how they want to handle a situation.

The **Are you going to make a Good Choice or a Bad Choice?** step gives your students the opportunity to decide what kind of choice they want to make. In real life situations in which students need to decide whether they are going to make a Good Choice or a Bad Choice, teachers generally tell their students what positive outcome or reinforcement will result when they make a Good Choice. They also tell their students what negative outcome or consequence will occur if they make a Bad Choice.

The next step, **What are your Choices or Steps?**, helps students develop a specific plan or approach for performing a social skill. Initially, it is at this step in the Stop & Think process that you will teach the steps of the social skill you are focusing on. Later, it is the step where students verbalize the steps aloud or to themselves.

For preschool to early elementary students, you will likely choose the appropriate social skill and guide your students through the Stop & Think steps. During this process, it is helpful to tell your students what they need to do and have them repeat what you've said. Thus, you will explicitly teach them the steps to the social skill and have them verbalize all the steps, so that they will internalize them over time.

The skill steps for the ten core and ten advanced skills selected for this manual are provided in the skill lessons in Part II. To teach any other skill, you need only identify the desired behavior, list the steps needed to perform the skill (using age-appropriate language and as few steps as possible), fit the steps into the Stop & Think language and process, and go for it!

To be implemented successfully, some social skills (e.g., Listening, Following Directions) require a very specific sequence of steps. These are called Step Skills. With other social skills (e.g., Dealing With Teasing), students can choose from a number of Good Choice options to successfully perform the skill. These skills are called Choice Skills. For both types of skills, the third step of the Stop & Think process prompts students to think about the sequence of steps needed to exhibit a particular social skill or the Good Choice options that could possibly resolve an existing situation.

Once your students have identified the Good Choices or steps needed for a particular situation and are prepared to demonstrate a specific social skill, the **Do It!** step naturally follows. The **Do It!** step is completed when the students actually carry out their plan, implement the social skill chosen, and evaluate whether the plan has worked. With younger students, especially when they are first learning a social skill, you may need to physically guide them through the skill, saying and modeling the steps one at a time. Even when older elementary school students are first practicing a new skill, it often helps when they repeat the skill steps out loud as they implement them. Over time, they will be able to say these steps silently and perform the skill more automatically.

If the **Do It!** step works, your students will be ready to go on to the final step, reinforcing themselves for doing a good job. Sometimes, however, a skill may not have the desired effect or result. If the skill is a Step Skill, the student needs to go back over the skill steps and practice them more carefully. If it is a Choice Skill, the student should be prompted to identify another social skill or to select a different Good Choice option. For example, if a group still doesn't want a "left out" student to join, then that student may have to decide to do something else.

Once successful with the **Do It!** step, a student can move on to the final step in the Stop & Think process. The **Good Job!** step prompts students to positively reinforce themselves for successfully using a social skill and successfully responding to a situation or request. This step is important because students do not always reinforce one another for making Good Choices and doing a good job and because adults may not be present to reinforce them. If you are a teacher of very young students, you will have to teach your students how to reinforce themselves. You can do this by patting them on the back (or giving them a hug) after they have done a good job and telling them that they did a good job. Immediately after, you would prompt them to tell themselves that they "did a good job" and have them pat themselves on the back. Over time, you will need to *only* prompt this last step and your students will do all of this automatically. Eventually, they will tell themselves that they did a good job without any prompting at all. This step helps students recognize when they have been successful and teaches them how to reinforce themselves for a job well done.

When used over time, the Stop & Think process helps you to teach your students how to (1) decrease their immediate, sometimes impulsive or emotional reactions to certain situations; (2) identify Good and Bad Choices and their respective outcomes and consequences; (3) demonstrate specific social skills for specific problem situations; (4) reinforce themselves when they have been successful.

Stop & Think Scripts

The following script shows how you might guide a student through the five Stop & Think steps when that student is not following a direction appropriately.

> Alex, you are not following my directions and cleaning up your area appropriately. You need to **Stop and Think**. **Are you going to make a Good Choice or a Bad Choice?** If you make a Good Choice and finish picking up your things, we will be ready for our Reading Circle and we can read one of your favorite stories to the class. If you make a Bad Choice and do not finish picking up your things, you will not be able to choose a story for today, and you will need to get ready for the Reading Circle early and before anyone else tomorrow. It's your choice. What do you want to do? [Wait for a response.] Great! I'm glad that you have decided to make a Good Choice. Now, **What are your Steps** so that you can finish this task? That's right, you need to (1) put all your materials into your desk, (2) throw all your trash into the trash can, and (3) sit in your seat in the "ready" position. Are you ready to **Do It**? **Do It!** [Wait for the student to finish.] **Good Job!** I like the way that you followed my directions so quickly and correctly. Are we ready for Reading Circle now? Are you thinking about a story you would like us to read?

Now, let's look at a script you could use if a student continues to make a Bad Choice and has to face the consequences.

> Alexandra, you are not following my directions and cleaning up your area appropriately. You need to **Stop and Think**. **Are you going to make a Good Choice or a Bad Choice?** If you make a Good Choice and finish picking up your things, we will be ready for our Reading Circle and we can read one of your favorite stories to the class. If you make a Bad Choice and do not finish picking up your things, you will not be able to choose a story for today and you will need to get ready for the Reading Circle early and before anyone else tomorrow. It's your choice. What do you want to do? [Student refuses to respond or doesn't pick up her things.] Alexandra, I'm sorry that you are continuing to make a Bad Choice. You will not be able to choose a story for today and, tomorrow, you will need to get ready for Reading Circle five minutes before anyone else. I hope that you will make a Good Choice right now and finish cleaning up your area in the next three minutes. Are you ready to **Do It**? **Do It!** [Wait for the student to begin cleaning up.] **Good Job!** I hope that tomorrow you will make a Good Choice and follow my directions the first time, even though you will be starting five minutes early.

It is important to note that while you want to encourage Good Choices as much as possible (remember the 5-to-1 Rule), there are times when you should allow a student to make a Bad Choice if he or she is determined to do so. This is especially true when you have meaningful and effective consequences in place for responding to these Bad Choices. For example, if a student does not follow directions when you ask her to return to her seat and get ready for the next activity, an effective solution would be to follow up this Bad Choice by escorting the student to her seat and later having her spend ten minutes of recess time practicing the **Following Directions** skill.

Students sometimes learn only when they experience the consequences for their Bad Choices. When your students realize that there are consequences and that you will consistently follow through with these consequences, they should begin to make more Good Choices automatically over time. It is important to note, however, that you should never let your students make Bad Choices when they could result in any physical or emotional danger or harm.

Finally, it is important to not use an excessively angry or loud voice when your students make Bad Choices and must receive a consequence. Instead, use a firm yet matter-of-fact voice. An angry or loud voice often triggers negative emotional responses that interfere with your primary goal: to get your students to make Good Choices.

To summarize, the five Stop & Think steps look like this:

1.

2.

3.

4.

5.

Many times, teachers communicate the Stop & Think steps by using hand signals as well as verbal signals. These signals are:

1. Putting your hand out like a police officer stopping traffic and then tilting your head and pointing with one finger to your cheek (**Stop and Think!**)

2. Giving your student a "thumbs up and thumbs down" and ending with a "thumbs up" (**Good Choice or Bad Choice?**—I want you to make a Good Choice!)

3. Putting both hands out to the side with palms up and shrugging your shoulders (**What are your Choices or Steps?**)

4. Putting your hand up in the air with fist clenched, then bringing that hand straight down toward your shoulder (**Do It!**)

5. Patting yourself on the back (**Good Job!**)

The Five-Step Teaching Process

As noted earlier, the steps for implementing a particular social skill are taught (and repeated or recited by students) in Step 3 of the Stop & Think process (**What are your Choices or Steps?**). Once these steps are taught, they are integrated into the five Stop & Think steps to form a **script**. Thereafter, the skill and script are always taught using the same teaching process, which involves:

1. **Teaching** the steps of the desired social skill

2. **Modeling** the steps and the social skills language (or script)

3. **Role playing** the steps and the script with your students, providing them practice opportunities

4. **Giving performance feedback** to your students as to how well they are doing with both the script and the new behavior

5. **Applying, and having your students use,** the skill and its steps as much as possible during the day to reinforce the teaching over time, in different settings, with different people, and in different situations

Teaching the steps of the desired social skill involves providing students with the steps and choices (if any) for implementing the skill and then integrating them into the Stop & Think script. These steps and choices are covered in Part II of this manual.

When **Modeling** a social skill, you need to clearly verbalize the Stop & Think steps (including the skill steps) while showing your students how to perform the desired behavior. That is, you need to clearly verbalize the skill *script*. As seen in the scripts already provided in this manual, a skill script tells your students, step by step, how to perform a specific social skill. The script is the key to the entire Stop & Think teaching process. Once your students are able to follow a skill's script, they will more easily demonstrate the social skill correctly and that skill will become part of their behavior. Once your students have practiced and are able to respond to your prompting of the social skill script, they will use the skill and script more independently and more successfully in different situations.

Bear in mind that you should always model only the appropriate or desired behavior when teaching a social skill; you should never demonstrate the inappropriate behavior as a way of teaching your students what not to do. Because you are trying to condition or recondition your students toward appropriate behavior, showing them inappropriate behavior will either weaken or confuse the positive or appropriate behavioral patterns that you are trying to teach and reinforce.

After modeling a new social skill for your students, have them practice or role play both the skill and the verbal script as many times a day as possible. Whenever you practice a skill with your students, make sure that they correctly verbalize the entire script, from the **Stop and Think!** step all the way to the **Good Job!** step. Remember, however, that at these age levels, your students will be repeating the scripts that you are verbally prompting.

The following is a script a student might repeat out loud with a teacher during a role play to demonstrate and eventually learn the **Listening** skill.

> Mrs. Jones wants us to listen carefully. I need to **Stop and Think! Am I going to make a Good Choice or a Bad Choice?** I want to make a Good Choice. **What are my Steps?** I need to (1) use my eyes, (2) put my hands in my lap, and (3) open my ears. I'm going to **Do It! Good Job!** I did a great job of listening.

Here is an example of a script for the **Following Directions** skill:

> Mr. Jiminez is going to give out a worksheet and some directions. He needs me to follow his directions. I need to **Stop and Think. Am I going to make a Good Choice or a Bad Choice?** I want to make a Good Choice. **What are my Steps** for **Following Directions**? I need to (1) listen to his directions, (2) ask a question if I don't understand, (3) repeat the direction to myself, and (4) get ready to follow the direction. Am I ready to **Do It**? Yes, here I go. **Good Job!** I did a great job of following the direction.

When practicing a social skill with younger students, remember that you will need to verbalize each part of the social skills script and have your students repeat each step out loud. You should then ask your students to follow your directions or cues and guide them through the desired behavior for each step. As students become more verbal and as their memories improve, they will be able to repeat and perform the scripts more independently over time. However, even older students will not always be able to verbalize and then memorize a social skills script the first time they learn it, especially for skills that are complex or that involve highly emotional situations. Thus, early in the teaching process, even teachers of middle to late elementary students need to have their students verbalize the socials skills scripts with them and when they are practicing.

Note that it is best to use role-play situations that occur in your classroom and school and, if possible, to practice these situations in the actual settings and with the real people involved. This will make the teaching and importance of using the skill more relevant and apparent to your students, will facilitate the students' use of the skill in the future, and will help students master these skills more quickly.

During role plays or other practice opportunities, you should **give performance feedback** to your students. There are two types of performance feedback, **formative** performance feedback and **summative** performance feedback. The former occurs during a role play if the student verbalizing the script or performing the skill begins to get off track. Here, the teacher stops the role play, provides corrective performance feedback, and restarts the role play. All of this ensures a positive practice of the skill and script. The latter occurs after a successful role play where the participants in the role play, the peers watching the role play, and the teacher provide positive feedback as to what made the role play and the practice of the skill successful.

Overall, performance feedback should positively reinforce the students for correctly (1) verbalizing the social skills script, (2) demonstrating the appropriate skill or behavior, and (3) reviewing their performance after the role play or practice session is over. In addition, feedback typically comes from the participants in the role play first (self-evaluation), then from the peer group, and then from the teacher. All feedback should be as specific and constructive as possible. For example, you might say, "Jesse, you did a really nice job of saying the four steps of the **Listening** skill while performing them for me."

If a student incorrectly verbalizes a social skills script or practices the wrong steps, your feedback should describe what he or she needs to do to correct the situation. You should then have the student practice the social skill and the skill script again, making sure that the correct script is used and the appropriate behaviors are demonstrated. Since students learn best when they repeatedly practice appropriate behaviors, this type of corrective feedback and practice will help to ensure that your teaching has the greatest (and quickest) impact on your students.

After the training is complete, make sure that you and your students use the social skills that have been taught as much as possible during the day. To do this, you need to be on the alert for "teachable moments," naturally occurring situations when you can practice or reinforce previously taught social skills scripts with your students.

There are three types of teachable moments. They occur (1) when students have successfully demonstrated an appropriate social skill and you can positively reinforce the verbal script that they probably used to attain this success; (2) when students have made a Bad Choice, by demonstrating an inappropriate social skill, giving you the opportunity to have them use the correct skill and verbal script to remediate the situation; and (3) when students are faced with a problem or situation that can be solved by choosing and using the appropriate social skill and script.

If you carry out all of these steps of the teaching process, your students will realize that you are going to consistently use and reinforce the social skills and the Stop & Think process. They should then begin to demonstrate the social skills that you are teaching more automatically and, as a result, begin to make more Good Choices.

Remember:

- **When Modeling**

    You need to make sure that your students . . .

    - have the prerequisite skills to be successful.
    - are taught using language that they can understand.
    - are taught in simple steps that ensure success.
    - hear the social skills script as you model the social skill behavior.

- **When Role Playing**

    You need to make sure that your students . . .

    - verbalize, repeat, or hear the social skills script as they demonstrate the appropriate behavior.
    - practice only the positive or appropriate social skill behavior.
    - receive ongoing and consistent practice opportunities.
    - use relevant practice situations that simulate the "emotional" intensity of the real situations so that they can respond to your social skill prompts and be able to demonstrate social skills under increasing conditions of emotionality.
    - are expected to practice the skills in a manner that is appropriate for their age level.

- **When Giving Performance Feedback**

    You need to make sure that the feedback is . . .

    - specific and descriptive.
    - provided to reinforce your students' successful use of the social skills script and demonstration of the social skill behavior, or to correct an inaccurate or incomplete social skills script or behavioral demonstration.
    - positive; focusing on what was done well and what can be done well (or better) the next time.

- **When Reinforcing or Applying the Skills After Practice**

    You need to make sure that you reinforce the social skills script and behavior when . .

    - your students have successfully demonstrated an appropriate social skill.

    - your students have made a Bad Choice, demonstrating an inappropriate social skill.

    - your students are faced with a problem or situation that can be solved by using the appropriate social skill and script.

    - your students must use the skill in situations that are different from those that you used when you taught and practiced the social skill.

Part II

Skill Lessons

A Two-Week Schedule for Teaching the Stop & Think Social Skills

Prior to beginning your first social skills lesson, it is important to introduce the Stop & Think process to your students through an introductory lesson. This lesson typically takes from 10 to 20 minutes for preschool students and from 20 to 30 minutes for first grade students, and occurs during Circle Time for preschoolers and at an opportune time for first graders. Typically, during this lesson, the following topics are discussed in developmentally appropriate ways: (1) What are social skills (or "Getting Along" skills or "Being a Good Friend" skills) and why are they important? (2) What are Good Choices and Bad Choices and what happens when we make each of them? (3) What are the advantages of making Good Choices and the disadvantages of making Bad Choices? (4) How will social skills be taught in the classroom? (5) What are the five steps of the Stop & Think process? The following is an outline of the introductory social skills lesson:

- *Step 1: General Discussion of What Social Skills Are*—This discussion should focus on ensuring that students know what social skills are and that they know the difference between Good Choice behavior and Bad Choice behavior.

- *Step 2: Discussion of Why It Is More Advantageous to Use Good Social Skills Than to Not Use Them*—Generally, students will want to talk about times when it is okay to not make a Good Choice, such as times when it is okay to fight. However, you should keep the focus on what happens to them when they do not use Good Choice behavior, particularly if they get caught. Keep the focus on "But what happens to you?"

- *Step 3: Discussion of Social Skills Behaviors That Your Students Might Want to Work on*—Here, ask your students what skills or behaviors, if they were present in the classroom, would make the classroom more relaxed, comfortable, or fun to be in, or would make it easier for everyone to get along with one another. Be sure to introduce this discussion with a developmentally appropriate question or in a developmentally appropriate context for your students. You might only have to ask, "What do you need to do in the classroom to be a good friend?"

- *Step 4: Overview of the Teaching Process—Modeling, Role Playing, Giving Performance Feedback, Transfer of Training*—Your focus here should be on making your students understand that the social skills lessons will be just like any other lesson. Explain that you will demonstrate the targeted skill and its steps, have the students practice it, provide feedback, and then have the students use the skill in the classroom and school when appropriate situations arise.

- *Step 5: Demonstration of the Stop & Think Steps*—Here, you will show students how the Stop & Think steps are used in practicing and carrying out a social skill.

After completing the introductory lesson, you will be ready to begin the formal teaching of specific social skills. The typical two-week teaching routine to be used for each skill is described in the following sections.

Phase 1: Teaching

On **Monday, Tuesday, and Wednesday (minimally) of the first week**, a social skills "class" is conducted during Circle Time in the morning and generally lasts for less than 25 minutes.

On **Monday**, introduce the social skill, discuss why the skill is important for your students, discuss where and when the skill should be demonstrated in the classroom and/or school, teach the skill and skill steps, model the skill (verbalizing the skill script), and do at least two role plays with the students involving situations that they identify as important times for using the skill in the classroom. A prototype of this instructional lesson might look like this:

- *Step 1: General Reminder of What Social Skills Are or General Introduction/Orientation to the Social Skills Lesson*—This should take about three minutes and should focus on introducing or reorienting students to the social skills lesson, process, and rules of instruction as needed or desired.

- *Step 2: Brief Reminder of Why Using Social Skills Is More Advantageous to Your Students Than Not Using Them*

- *Step 3: Introduction of the Social Skill to Be Taught*—Here, you would (1) provide a context for the skill—that is, explaining why it is important, what happens if a student does or does not demonstrate the skill, and when the skill should be demonstrated; (2) conduct a discussion of what steps or choices should make up the skill; and (3) have the class generate some classroom or school-based situations when the skill might be needed or used.

- *Step 4: Review of the Stop & Think Steps, Integrating the Steps or Choices for the Social Skill Being Taught Into Step 3*

- *Step 5: Teaching of the New Social Skill—Modeling, Role Playing, and Giving Performance Feedback—* At a minimum, do one modeling demonstration and have your students do at least two role plays. Additional role plays are done during the social skills lesson time during the next two days.

- *Step 6: Summary, Transfer of Training, and Integration of the New Skill Into the Existing Classroom Incentive System—* Here, you would discuss how, where, and when you expect your students to use the skill during a routine classroom day.

On **Tuesday**, review the social skill and skill steps and then move into role plays with your students.

On **Wednesday**, again review the social skill and skill steps and then move into additional role plays with your students. The ultimate goal of these teaching lessons and role plays is to make sure that every student in the classroom has as many opportunities as possible to be prompted by the teacher and to repeat and verbalize the entire script for the social skill being taught (so that you can reinforce the student if the script is verbalized correctly or correct the student if it is verbalized incorrectly). Just as with an academic or academic readiness lesson, feel free to vary your approaches and teaching formats to the role plays. For example, the role plays can involve individual students, small cooperative or play groups, large groups, the entire class, and anything in between. Thus, these role plays do not always have to be one-on-one situations. Games, center-based activities, and other teaching/role-play approaches can be used. Use your creativity and teaching expertise when planning the role plays.

Throughout the teaching lessons, be sure to adapt the teaching process to take into account your students' developmental level and needs. For example, you might use puppets or other adaptations for the role plays and visual symbols, icons, or signs instead of writing for the skill steps.

Phase 2: Application Activities

Once you have accomplished the goals for teaching a new social skill, you are ready to move on to application activities. These activities are generally conducted on the three days following the teaching lessons (i.e., Thursday, Friday, and the next Monday and possibly Tuesday) and involve a 15- to 25-minute period *during the routine academic day* where the social skill is integrated into an academic, preacademic, or social/interactional lesson. (For some skills, you may want to include school-based situations [e.g., during P.E., in the cafeteria] in your application activities.) While this integration may be somewhat artificial, the application activities give students the opportunity to practice the social skill and script in the context of the daily classroom routine. Over time, this process gives students more chances to practice the social skill and the skill script and helps the students to transfer their social skills training into real settings and situations. With all application activities, be sure that your students are correctly carrying out the skill steps, verbalizing the skill script after your prompts, and using the entire Stop & Think process.

An example of an application activity for the **Following Directions** skill is to conduct a typical seatwork lesson and tell your students that they will practice the script for **Following Directions** three to four times as prompted by their teacher as they complete the tasks of the lesson. With this, as with any application activity, the goal is to have your students consciously practice the skill in a more real-life situation in the classroom, so that they can move closer to mastering the skill and performing it more automatically.

There are two additional benefits to these application activities. First, while the application activities provide students with much-needed practice, they do not require more lessons that take time away from your academic schedule. Second, having students practice and use the **Following Directions** skill during an academic or preacademic or social/interactional lesson will help them to be more successful during the lesson itself and should decrease the time you spend correcting students for not following academic directions. Similar benefits will be obtained with the practice of other skills.

When planning application times and opportunities, it is best to begin by using classroom activities in which the skill is most easily and successfully integrated and practiced. Over time, you can use other activities during the day where the use of the skill is more challenging for the students involved. And, once again, you may use building-based activities to further practice and transfer your skills.

Phase 3: Infusion Opportunities

During **the last three or four days of the second week**, prompt and reinforce your students at every reasonable opportunity for using the social skill and the script that was taught and reinforced during the past week and a half. Here, it is important to look for teachable moments—situations during which the social skill can be naturally practiced and/or reinforced. You might, for example, ask a student who has successfully used the social skill to verbalize with you the script he or she used to facilitate this success. Or, upon seeing an opportunity for a student to use the skill and avoid making a Bad Choice, you might prompt the student to verbalize the skill script and demonstrate how he or she would make a Good Choice. Although you may provide special incentives for students to identify opportunities to use and practice the script during these three days, the goal is to have your students use the social skill as naturally as possible and as often as is necessary in the classroom, moving them even further toward the highest degree of skill independence and mastery for their developmental level.

Summary

As described in this section, when teaching social skills with the Stop & Think process, you may have to conduct only three actual social skills lessons for any social skill introduced. These lessons should be followed by activities in which the social skill is applied in a more "normal" classroom setting and then by the ongoing reinforcement of the skill as it occurs naturally in the classroom and school. You may, of course, teach more lessons if desired (and this is encouraged), but three may be enough with the recommended application and infusion follow-through.

Specific role-play, application, and infusion activities for each of the ten core skills are suggested in the skill lessons that follow. These activities involve situations that commonly occur in most classrooms. You should, however, add or substitute your own activities to address any concerns you may have related to your own students, classroom, and school situation.

A sample lesson plan that you can use for teaching the core skills, or any other social skills, is included in the *Stop & Think Reproducible Forms*. Remember, to teach a skill not included in this manual, you need only identify the desired behavior; list the steps needed to perform the skill (using age-appropriate language and as few steps as possible); determine role-play, application, and infusion opportunities; and then go for it! Virtually any social skill can be effectively taught within the Stop & Think process.

SKILL 1

Listening

Listening is the most basic skill for all school students and the first skill taught in the Stop & Think process. At the preschool level, **Listening** begins as an "orienting response"—that is, students are taught to get into the listening position (making eye contact, body facing you, ears open), so that listening naturally follows. At the early elementary level, students actually learn the process of listening. Because students are expected to listen for longer periods of time and to more complex information as they get older, **Listening** is a skill that teachers should never stop teaching or reviewing with their students.

Phase 1: Teaching
(Generally, Monday, Tuesday, and Wednesday of Week 1)

To teach this skill (and all other skills as well), first ask your students to **Stop and Think**. Then ask if they **are going to make a Good Choice or a Bad Choice**. Once they have decided to make a Good Choice, begin to teach them the **Listening** skill.

For younger students (generally, preschool and kindergarten), teach the following **Steps** for the **Listening** skill:

1. **Eyes**—Look at the person who is talking.

2. **Hands**—Put your hands in your lap (or on your table or by your sides) and get into the listening position.

3. **Ears**—Hear what is being said to you.

For older elementary students (generally, first grade), teach these **Steps**:

1. **Look** at the person who is talking.

2. **Listen** to and **think** about what is being said.

3. If needed, **ask** a question.

4. When appropriate, **say** what you want or need to say.

Once your students are ready to demonstrate the **Listening** skill, ask them to **Do It**. When your students are successful, have them pat themselves on the back and say **"Good Job!"**

Remember to teach this and every social skill using the same teaching process. This process involves:

1. **Teaching** the steps of the desired social skill

2. **Modeling** the steps and the social skills language (or script)

3. **Role playing** the steps and the language with your students, providing them practice opportunities

4. **Giving performance feedback** to your students as to how accurately they are performing both the script and the new behavior

5. **Applying, and having your students use,** the skill and its steps as much as possible during the day to reinforce the teaching over time, in different settings, with different people, and in different situations

As you initially model, role play, and have your students apply this skill during the day, it is important to choose situations where (1) the skill will be used frequently, (2) the skill will be noticeable—by peers as well as by you and other adults, (3) the skill will be viewed positively, (4) many different people will reinforce your students, and (5) your students are likely to succeed.

Finally, as you plan practice situations for the **Listening** skill, think about when and where your students already demonstrate this behavior. Also, think about situations where you wish your students would demonstrate the behavior.

Suggested Role Plays for This Skill

There are many situations in which the **Listening** skill should be used in the classroom, and it is a good idea to have students role play a variety of them when they are learning and practicing the **Listening** skill and script. The following are some of these situations:

- Listening when you are providing whole-group instruction, such as instruction on ABC's or days of the week

- Listening when you are using puppets for instruction

- Listening when you are providing directions to the class

- Listening when you are reading a story to the class

- Listening when you are providing directions to an individual student, such as asking a student to deliver a message, complete a class activity or task, or act as the classroom helper

- Listening to directions for a complex task

- Listening when you redirect a student who is daydreaming, behaving inappropriately, talking out of turn, or emotionally upset

- Listening to another student or students when they are engaging in play activities, sharing, providing assistance, or working with a partner

You are encouraged to think about the role-play situations that would be most beneficial for your own students and class. As you do so, feel free to add to or modify this list. Then, jot down your list on your lesson plan for teaching the **Listening** skill.

Teaching Tips

The two sets of **Listening** skill steps recommended in this lesson are based on the feedback of teachers across the country. While your students will most likely be successful using one of these two sets of steps, it is important to note that you can change or make up your own steps to the **Listening** skill, or any other social skill, as needed. The key is to make sure that the language and number of steps are appropriate for the age and developmental level of your students.

Whichever set of **Listening** skill steps you teach, it is helpful to pair the steps over time with a verbal cue, such as "Show me **Listening**," or a physical cue, such as a tug on your ear. Over time, this will decrease your need to verbalize all of the skill steps when practicing the skill, and it will help your students to internalize the skill steps while demonstrating the expected behavior. Eventually, you will be able to tell your students to show you listening, or tug on your ear, and they will immediately get into the listening position (eye contact, body facing you, and ears open).

As you use the Stop & Think process to teach **Listening** to your students, always remember to carry out the last of the Stop & Think steps by telling your students that they have done a **Good Job** and by patting them on the back or giving them a hug. Over time, your students should pat themselves on the back, telling *themselves* **Good Job!** This is important because as students get older (1) they will need to learn to reinforce themselves; (2) they will need to increasingly depend on their own feedback, as fewer and fewer adults will be nearby to provide reinforcement; and (3) this self-reinforcement will become an important component of their positive self-esteem.

Phase 2: Application Activities
(Generally, Thursday and Friday of Week 1 and Monday and Tuesday of Week 2)

Remember that the purpose of your application activities is to integrate the social skill that has just been taught into regular academic, preacademic, or social/interactional lessons. Your goals with application activities are (1) to give your students more opportunities to practice the skill and script, and (2) to give this practice in more real-life classroom and, perhaps, building situations. The application activities are usually conducted over a 15- to 25-minute period during a regular academic, preacademic, or social/interactional lesson on the three or four days following the teaching of the skill.

Before having your students engage in a classroom-based application activity for **Listening**, remind them that they will be repeating the steps to the **Listening** skill and the skill script with you during the activity. Examples of classroom-based application activities for preschool to early elementary students include:

- Reminding the class to use the **Listening** skill when it is time to line up (e.g., for an out-of-class activity, lunch, or fire drills)
- Having students practice the **Listening** skill when you instruct them to move to or from classroom learning centers, when they are involved in activities in the learning centers, and when you are instructing them to clean up following learning center activities
- Reminding the class to use the **Listening** skill during whole-group instruction, such as when you are reading aloud, when they are using manipulatives, or when you are demonstrating lessons
- Having the class use the **Listening** skill when guests are in the classroom

Remember that these are just suggestions. It is important to carefully consider your own classroom situation, then list appropriate application activities for your students on your lesson plan.

Phase 3: Infusion Opportunities
(Generally, the Rest of Week 2)

Infusion opportunities are naturally occurring teachable moments that give students the chance to practice their social skills. Be alert for situations in which students should and do or don't use **Listening**, and provide prompts and feedback to reinforce the positive use of the skill and its script.

Note that teachable moments for **Listening** occur throughout the school, not just in the classroom. For example, students should use the **Listening** skill when they are with adults in the hallway, at recess, in the cafeteria, at assemblies, on field trips, and riding the bus. They can also use this skill when adults are helping them resolve arguments or disagreements.

Take some time now to consider your students' classroom and school situations, and then list likely infusion opportunities for your students on your lesson plan.

Social Skills Cue Cards

Stop & Think Reproducible Forms contains social skills cue cards (that you will want to reproduce for your students) for every core and advanced social skill discussed in this manual. The cue card for each skill lists the specific steps that you and your students need to follow when using that skill with the Stop & Think process. Also included in *Reproducible Forms* are a number of "Stop & Think Stop Signs" and "Stop & Think Step Signs" (listing the five steps of the Stop & Think process). Put the "Stop Signs" and "Step Signs" in strategic places in your classroom and around your school. All these aids serve as reminders to your students that you want them to make Good Choices so that the Stop & Think process can work well for all of you.

(For Younger Students)

Listening
Skill 1
PreK-1: **CORE**

 1. **Eyes** — Look at the person who is talking.

 2. **Hands** — Put your hands on your lap (or on your table or by your sides) and get into the listening position.

 3. **Ears** — Hear what is being said to you.

The Stop & Think Social Skills Program © 2001 by Sopris West. All rights reserved. To order: 800-547-6747. Code 102CARDPRE.

(For Older Students)

Listening
Skill 1
PreK-1: **CORE**

 1. **Look** at the person who is talking.

 2. **Listen** to and **think** about what is being said.

 3. If needed, **ask** a question.

 4. When appropriate, **say** what you want or need to say.

The Stop & Think Social Skills Program © 2001 by Sopris West. All rights reserved. To order: 800-547-6747. Code 102CARDPRE.

Part II: Skill Lessons

SKILL 2
Following Directions

If **Listening** is the most basic skill for all students, then **Following Directions** is the second most basic skill. This is because students initially learn most things by modeling or imitating others while following their directions and then by trying to do those things themselves. If students are unable to follow directions effectively, they may learn new things incorrectly, ineffectively, or not at all. In addition, if they are unable to follow directions, they will have a difficult time learning new academic skills and the more advanced Stop & Think social skills that they need for ongoing success. Thus, the **Following Directions** skill is vital if additional skills are to be learned.

Phase 1: Teaching
(Generally, Monday, Tuesday, and Wednesday of Week 1)

To teach this skill, first ask your students to **Stop and Think**, and then ask if they **are going to make a Good Choice or a Bad Choice**. Once they have decided to make a Good Choice, begin to teach them the **Following Directions** skill.

The **Steps** that students need to follow to learn and demonstrate the **Following Directions** skill are:

1. **Listen** to the direction.

2. **Ask** a question if needed or if you don't understand.

3. **Repeat** the direction out loud or to yourself.

4. Get ready to **follow** the direction.

Once your students are ready to demonstrate **Following Directions**, ask them to **Do It!** When your students are successful, have them pat themselves on the back and say, "**Good Job!**"

Remember to teach this and every social skill using the same teaching process. This process involves:

1. **Teaching** the steps of the desired social skill

2. **Modeling** the steps and the social skills language (or script)

3. **Role playing** the steps and the language with your students, providing them practice opportunities

4. **Giving performance feedback** to your students as to how accurately they are performing both the script and the new behavior

5. **Applying, and having your students use,** the skill and its steps as much as possible during the day to reinforce the teaching over time, in different settings, with different people, and in different situations

As you initially model, role play, and have your students apply this skill during the day, it is important to choose situations where (1) the skill will be used frequently, (2) the skill will be noticeable—by peers as well as by you and other adults, (3) the skill will be viewed positively, (4) many different people will reinforce your students, and (5) your students are likely to succeed.

Finally, as you plan practice situations for the **Following Directions** skill, think about when and where your students already demonstrate this behavior. Also, think about situations where you wish they would demonstrate the behavior.

Suggested Role Plays for This Social Skill

Students need to follow directions throughout the school day. There are an endless number of role-play scenarios, and it is a good idea to have students role play a variety of them when they are learning and practicing the **Following Directions** skill. The following are some of these situations:

- Following the directions to sit down or stand up quietly
- Following the directions to walk appropriately in the classroom or hallway
- Following the directions to sit appropriately in Circle Time or in a classroom center
- Following the directions for performing or practicing a new academic or preacademic skill

You are encouraged to think about the role-play situations that would be most beneficial for your own students and class. As you do so, feel free to add to or modify this list. Then, jot down your list on your lesson plan for teaching **Following Directions**.

Teaching Tips

The **Following Directions** steps listed here are the same as those taught to middle and late elementary school students. However, the older students are expected to respond positively to more complex, more varied, and longer directions. To help prepare your students for what is ahead, slowly increase your expectations for following directions over time and continually practice the **Following Directions** skill with them.

When teaching the **Following Directions** skill (as well as all of the other social skills), it is important to use language that your students understand and to make sure that they are able to easily follow the number of steps that you provide in your directions. Keep everything simple and concrete. Preschool to early elementary students typically are able to follow one-, two-, or possibly three-step directions. However, when they are under stress (e.g., angry, anxious, frustrated, or tired), their ability to effectively follow the social skill steps and the directions you provide often decreases.

In addition, bear in mind the following three principles related to choosing and using the skill steps for any social skill. First, as noted in the **Listening** skill lesson, it does not matter what specific teaching steps you use to teach a social skill. While the steps in this manual have been used and tested by teachers across the country, they may not fit your particular classroom or school situation. All of the scripts can be adapted or changed. What *does* matter—as noted earlier—is that (1) you use language and steps that your students can understand, (2) you do not use so many steps that you confuse or overwhelm your students, and (3) you consistently use the same steps every time that you practice or use the skill.

The second principle is to use skill steps that can be easily communicated and remembered. Ideally, and over time, you will want to collapse these steps into one-word or short sentence prompts so that you can cue the behavior you want without having to go through all of the steps out loud. For example, you eventually should be able to guide your students through the **Following Directions** script by saying something like, "You need to **Listen**, **Ask**, **Repeat**, and **Follow** the direction."

Third, you may have to physically guide your younger students the first few times after you give a new direction or teach a new social skill. Over time, you should pair your directions with a verbal or physical prompt (e.g., a key word or phrase, a hand motion or signal) so that you can eventually "cue" your students with the prompt rather than give the entire set of directions.

Phase 2: Application Activities
(Generally, Thursday and Friday of Week 1 and Monday and Tuesday of Week 2)

Remember that the purpose of your application activities is to integrate the social skill that has just been taught into regular academic, preacademic, or social/interactional lessons. Your goals with application activities are (1) to give your students more opportunities to practice the skill and script as prompted by you, and (2) to give this practice in more real-life classroom and, perhaps, building situations. The application activities are usually conducted over a 15- to 25-minute period during a regular academic, preacademic, or social/interactional lesson on the three or four days following the teaching of the skill.

Before having your students engage in a classroom-based application activity for **Following Directions**, remind them that they will be repeating the steps to the **Following Directions** skill and the skill script with you during the activity. Examples of classroom-based tasks or activities in which students can practice the **Following Directions** skill and script include the following:

- Games such as "Simon Says" that provide students with opportunities to practice following directions

- Academic tasks that involve multistep directions, such as "Everyone please take your books out, turn to page 15, and show me Listening"

- Coloring or number tasks, worksheets, penmanship or letter-writing practice, and other activities that require students to follow step-by-step directions

Remember that these are just suggestions. It is important to carefully consider your own classroom situation, then list appropriate application activities for your students on your lesson plan.

Phase 3: Infusion Opportunities
(Generally, the Rest of Week 2)

Infusion opportunities are naturally occurring teachable moments that give students the chance to practice their social skills. Students are constantly being asked to follow directions, both in and outside the classroom. Be alert for situations in which students should and do or don't use the **Following Directions** skill and provide prompts and feedback to reinforce the positive use of the skill and its script. Indeed, whenever students do not follow directions in the classroom (e.g., when a student runs instead of walks or when a student fails to take his or her seat as instructed), you should use the opportunity to review the Stop & Think **Following Directions** steps. Another infusion opportunity occurs when you use the **Follow Directions** skill and script as an "advanced organizer" for your students relative to them then completing a multistep behavior, activity, or academic task.

Take some time now to consider your students' classroom and school situation, and then list likely infusion opportunities for your students on your lesson plan.

Social Skills Cue Cards

The following is a copy of the cue card for the **Following Directions** skill. This cue card lists the specific steps that you and your students need to follow when using this skill within the Stop & Think process.

Remember, you will find cue cards for all of the core and advanced skills discussed in the manual in *Stop & Think Reproducible Forms* along with a number of "Stop & Think Stop Signs" and "Stop & Think Step Signs." Put the cue cards, "Stop Signs," and "Step Signs" in strategic places in your classroom and around your school and give a cue card to each of your students. All of these aids provide reminders to your students that you want them to make Good Choices so that the Stop & Think process can work well for all of you.

Following Directions Skill 2

PreK-1: CORE

 1. **Listen** to the direction.

 2. **Ask** a question if needed or if you don't understand.

 3. **Repeat** the direction out loud or to yourself.

 4. Get ready to **follow** the direction.

The Stop & Think Social Skills Program © 2001 by Sopris West. All rights reserved. To order: 800-547-6747. Code 102CARDPRE.

SKILL 3

Using Nice Talk

Using Nice Talk is a very important skill for all students. Clearly, teachers and other adults generally are more willing to consider a student's request when it is presented in a nice way as opposed to when it is presented in an angry, loud, whiny, or frustrated way. In addition, conflict situations between students and peers or students and teachers can often be defused when a nice voice, rather than an angry voice, is used.

Another reason to teach the **Using Nice Talk** skill is to help counteract the influence of the many poor role models that your students see each day on TV and in real life—actors and others who do not speak appropriately to adults or to peers or are quick to engage in interactions that involve conflict or aggression. You need to teach your students that there is a better way to interact, one that is positive and does not promote conflict.

Phase 1: Teaching
(Generally, Monday, Tuesday, and Wednesday of Week 1)

To teach this skill, first ask your students to **Stop and Think**, and then ask if they **are going to make a Good Choice or a Bad Choice**. Once they have decided to make a Good Choice, begin to teach them the **Using Nice Talk** skill.

The **Steps** that students need to follow to learn and demonstrate the **Using Nice Talk** skill are:

1. **Look** at the person you want to talk to

2. **Think** about what you want to say.

3. **Keep** your hands by your sides and **use** a friendly face.

4. **Say** what you want to say in a friendly way.

Once your students are ready to demonstrate **Using Nice Talk**, ask them to **Do It!** When your students are successful, have them pat themselves on the back and say, "**Good Job!**"

Remember to teach this and every social skill using the same teaching process. This process involves:

1. **Teaching** the steps of the desired social skill

2. **Modeling** the steps and the social skills language (or script)

3. **Role playing** the steps and the language with your students, providing them practice opportunities

4. **Giving performance feedback** to your students as to how accurately they are performing both the script and the new behavior

5. **Applying, and having your students use,** the skill and its steps as much as possible during the day to reinforce the teaching over time, in different settings, with different people, and in different situations

As you initially model, role play, and have your students apply this skill during the day, it is important to choose situations where (1) the skill will be used frequently, (2) the skill will be noticeable—by peers as well as by you and other adults, (3) the skill will be viewed positively, (4) many different people will reinforce your students, and (5) your students are likely to succeed.

Finally, as you plan practice situations for the **Using Nice Talk** skill, think about when and where your students already demonstrate this behavior. Also, think about situations where you wish they would demonstrate the behavior.

Suggested Role Plays for This Social Skill

Students should **Use Nice Talk** throughout the day in the classroom and school. Thus, the number of role-play situations is virtually unlimited. Following are some of the many possible role plays for this skill:

- Using nice talk when communicating with another student or with you

- Using nice talk when working in small groups

- Using nice talk when playing during free time

- Using nice talk when telling someone not to fight

- Using nice talk when asking for something

- Using nice talk when requesting help from a peer

You are encouraged to think about the role-play situations that would be most beneficial for your own students and class. As you do so, feel free to add to or modify this list. Then, jot down your list on your lesson plan for teaching **Using Nice Talk**.

Teaching Tips

Before teaching this skill, it is helpful to monitor how students and staff throughout your school talk to one another in different situations. If you find that your school as a whole is not using enough nice talk, your students will not have enough role models reinforcing the use of the skill and will probably have difficulty learning it. Further, if students and adults in the school are not using nice talk, you will have a hard time holding your students accountable for its use.

In such situations, you may want to suggest making the teaching and use of this skill a school project. Not only will you be encouraging everyone to use nice talk, but you will also be encouraging the use of the Stop & Think process, which is something that everyone in your school can benefit from.

In addition, be sure to demonstrate the **Using Nice Talk** skill at every possible opportunity during the day. For example, you can use nice talk when giving directions to students, when asking students to do something they don't want to do, when asking a student to pick something up, when delivering consequences, and when communicating with a colleague. When demonstrating these situations for students, be sure to point out how you are using the **Using Nice Talk** skill and script.

Phase 2: Application Activities
(Generally, Thursday and Friday of Week 1 and Monday and Tuesday of Week 2)

Remember that the purpose of your application activities is to integrate the social skill that has just been taught into regular academic, preacademic, or social/interactional lessons. Your goals with application activities are (1) to give your students more opportunities to practice the skill and script as prompted by you, and (2) to give this practice in more real-life classroom and, perhaps, building situations. The application activities are usually conducted over a 15- to 25-minute period during a regular academic, preacademic, or social/interactional lesson on the three or four days following the teaching of the skill.

Before having your students engage in a classroom-based application activity for **Using Nice Talk**, remind them that they will be repeating the steps to the **Using Nice Talk** skill and the skill script with you during the activity. Classroom-based tasks or activities in which students can practice the **Using Nice Talk** skill and script occur throughout the school day. Some examples include the following:

- Asking for paper, pencils, or other supplies
- Asking an adult for permission to do something
- Asking a peer to make a Good Choice
- Inviting a peer to a classroom center or to play a game
- Telling someone to stop pushing or interrupting

Remember that these are just suggestions. It is important to carefully consider your own classroom situation, then list appropriate application activities for your students on your lesson plan.

Phase 3: Infusion Opportunities
(Generally, the Rest of Week 2)

Infusion opportunities are naturally occurring teachable moments that give students the chance to practice their social skills. Be alert for situations in which students should and do or don't use nice talk and provide prompts and feedback to reinforce the positive use of the skill and its script.

Note that teachable moments for **Using Nice Talk** occur throughout the school, not just in the classroom. For example, students should use this skill when they are on the playground, on field trips, at assemblies, or in the cafeteria. They should also use this skill during academic free time and when talking with guests visiting the classroom.

Take some time now to consider your students' classroom and school situation, and then list likely infusion opportunities for your students on your lesson plan.

Social Skills Cue Cards

The following is a copy of the cue card for the **Using Nice Talk** skill. This cue card lists the specific steps that you and your students need to follow when using this skill within the Stop & Think process.

Remember, you will find cue cards for all of the core and advanced skills discussed in the manual in *Stop & Think Reproducible Forms*, along with a number of "Stop & Think Stop Signs" and "Stop & Think Step Signs." Put the cue cards "Stop Signs," and "Step Signs" in strategic places in your classroom and around your school and give a cue card to each of your students. All of these aids provide reminders to your students that you want them to make Good Choices so that the Stop & Think process can work well for all of you.

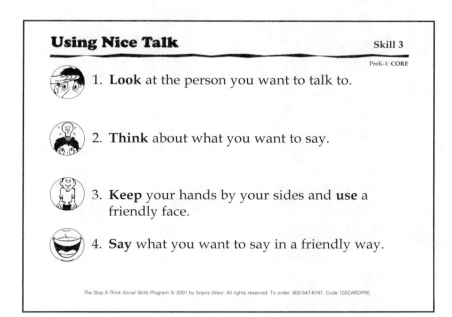

SKILL 4
Asking for Help

If preschool to early elementary school students are to be successful in school (as well as in all other settings), they need to know how to ask for help appropriately. Indeed, among many possible situations, this skill can help them when they are learning or practicing a new academic skill (e.g., when they are completing a worksheet), when they need help to solve a personal problem (e.g., when they need to use the bathroom, are thirsty, or are being bothered by a distraction), and when they need help to resolve a potential interpersonal problem (e.g., when a peer is not sharing or is teasing them). Over time, the **Asking for Help** skill will continue to be important as your students learn and practice new and more complex skills, experience increasing academic or interpersonal demands, and are confronted with safety-related situations for which they need help.

With regard to the latter, it is important to recognize that your students may face dangerous situations that they can't solve alone. When they are lost, when a stranger approaches them, when someone touches them inappropriately, and in other situations, use of the **Asking for Help** skill can mean the difference between a safe resolution to the problem and an unfortunate ending. Thus, it is critical that you extend practice of the **Asking for Help** skill from "routine" classroom situations to more extraordinary school situations and to more complex out-of-school situations.

By teaching the **Asking for Help** skill, you can help your students feel comfortable and competent in their ability to ask for your or others' assistance. Moreover, teaching this skill will help you maintain a positive relationship and an open communication style with your students—something that is increasingly important as students get older.

Two different sets of steps for the **Asking for Help** skill are presented below. Students would use the first set to ask for help when they are sitting at their desks or elsewhere. They would use the second set when they need to approach someone for assistance.

Phase 1: Teaching
(Generally, Monday, Tuesday, and Wednesday of Week 1)

To teach the **Asking for Help** skill using either set of steps, first ask your students to **Stop and Think**, and then ask if they **are going to make a Good Choice or a Bad Choice**. Once they have decided to make a Good Choice, begin to teach them the **Asking for Help** skill.

The **Steps** that students need to follow for **Asking for Help** when they are sitting at their desks are:

1. **Decide** if you really need to ask for help.

2. **Raise** your hand and **look** at the person you want help from.

3. **Wait** until you are recognized.

4. **Say**, "I need help," in a nice or quiet voice and **tell** the person what you need help with.

The **Steps** that students need to follow when they need to approach someone to **Ask for Help** are:

1. **Walk** up to the person you want help from.

2. **Look** at the person and **cue** the person to get his or her attention.

3. **Wait** until you are recognized.

4. **Say**, "I need help," in a nice or quiet voice and **tell** the person what you need help with.

Once your students are ready to demonstrate the **Asking for Help** skill, ask them to **Do It!** When your students are successful, have them pat themselves on the back and say, "**Good Job!**"

Remember to teach this and every social skill using the same teaching process. This process involves:

1. **Teaching** the steps of the desired social skill

2. **Modeling** the steps and the social skills language (or script)

3. **Role playing** the steps and the language with your students, providing them practice opportunities

4. **Giving performance feedback** to your students as to how accurately they are performing both the script and the new behavior

5. **Applying, and having your students use,** the skill and its steps as much as possible during the day to reinforce the teaching over time, in different settings, with different people, and in different situations

As you initially model, role play, and have your students apply this skill during the day, it is important to choose situations where (1) the skill will be used frequently, (2) the skill will be noticeable—by peers as well as by you and other adults, (3) the skill will be viewed positively, (4) many different people will reinforce your students, and (5) your students are likely to succeed.

Finally, as you plan practice situations for the **Asking for Help** skill, think about when and where your students already demonstrate this behavior. Also think about situations where you wish your students would demonstrate the behavior.

Suggested Role Plays for This Social Skill

There are many different situations in which students need to ask for help in and outside the classroom, and it is a good idea to have students role play a variety of these situations when learning and practicing the **Asking for Help** skill. Following are some of these situations:

- Asking for help in going to the bathroom
- Asking for help with a runny nose
- Asking for help when they have a broken pencil
- Asking for help finding a book bag or other school supplies they have misplaced
- Asking for help when they have not been picked up by a parent or have missed their bus
- Asking for help when they (or another student) are being teased, taunted, or bullied on the playground
- Asking for help when scared or alarmed
- Asking for help in a dangerous situation

You are encouraged to think about the role-play situations that would be most beneficial for your own students and class. As you do so, feel free to add to or modify this list. Then, jot down your list on your lesson plan for teaching the **Asking for Help** skill.

Teaching Tips

It is important to note that the way that students ask for help often determines your willingness to respond to them and sometimes even determines how you respond. Indeed, aren't you more willing to give a student a break or the benefit of the doubt when he or she asks for help in a nice way? Of course you are! And so are others! Thus, when you teach this skill to your students, it is important to reinforce the step that instructs students to ask for help with a nice or quiet voice. If a student asks for help in an angry or demanding way, he or she needs to practice using a friendly or quiet voice.

In addition to teaching your students how to use this skill, you also need to teach them when to use it. For example, if a student runs to you for help after making a Bad Choice, the student needs to practice when to use this skill (i.e., *before* making a Bad Choice). If you do not correct this behavioral pattern, you may actually end up *reinforcing* both the student's Bad Choice and his or her inappropriate request for help *after* the Bad Choice.

Further, you do not want to make your students dependent on you by encouraging them to use this skill when they don't really need the help. Thus, you may want to identify with your students the things that you and they know they can do independently. Then, when they are at the **Good Choice or Bad Choice** step of the Stop & Think process, you can teach them to say, "A Good Choice is to try this (job, task, activity, work) one more time and then to ask for help only when I am sure I really need it. A Bad Choice is to ask for help when I know that I can really do this (job, task, activity, work)."

Later, if a student does come to you for help, you need to decide (1) if the task really is too difficult for the student, (2) if the student can learn how to do the task within a short period of time, or (3) if the student can learn how to do the task right at that moment.

In the first situation, you should complete the task, but you may want to verbalize for the student the steps for doing so. This will make your student familiar with the sequence and steps needed to complete the task, preparing the student for the time when he or she will be ready to learn and complete the task independently.

In the second situation, you may want to model the task for the student (while also verbalizing the steps) and then have the student attempt the task with your verbal and physical guidance. Using this approach and with more step-by-step practice and success, the student should be able to do the task increasingly on his or her own until such time that he or she has mastered the steps and can do them independently.

The third situation typically involves a new task for the student but one that he or she can learn right away with your assistance. In such cases, you may simply want to positively reinforce the student for appropriately **Asking for Help** and then teach the task to the student, verbally and physically guiding him or her to success.

To make this more concrete, think about the process needed to teach first graders where to put their name on a worksheet and begin independent seatwork—and think about how often these students would ask you for help if you didn't teach this skill the right way. In the beginning, the task has too many steps and things for your students to remember (e.g., "Write your name on the paper's top line to the right, read the first problem, solve it, and check your answer"), so you guide your students through each step, one by one. Soon, however, your students are ready to learn and remember this process, and you guide them through the steps to mastery. Eventually, your students are ready to write their names and begin their seatwork independently, and you simply verbally prompt the process when they have a worksheet in front of them. At this point, you need only reinforce them for starting the work on their own and not needing to ask for help.

Phase 2: Application Activities
(Generally, Thursday and Friday of Week 1 and Monday and Tuesday of Week 2)

Remember that the purpose of your application activities is to integrate the social skill that has just been taught into regular academic, preacademic, or social/interactional lessons. Your goals with application activities are (1) to give your students more opportunities to practice the skill and script as prompted by you, and (2) to give this practice in more real-life classroom and, perhaps, building situations. The application activities are usually conducted over a 15- to 25-minute period during a regular academic, preacademic, and social/interactional lesson on the three or four days following the teaching of the skill.

Before having your students engage in a classroom-based application activity for **Asking for Help**, remind them that they will be repeating the steps to the **Asking for Help** skill and the skill script with you during the activity. Examples of classroom-based tasks or activities in which students can practice the **Asking for Help** skill and script include the following:

- Playing games such as "Mother May I," "Teacher May I," and "Police Officer May I" that require students to ask for help

- Having students select cards (on which you have written scenarios involving the need to ask for help) from a hat, read the scenario to the class, and then act it out

- Having students work on a task or problem but not giving them enough information to complete the task or solve the problem without asking for help

- Reading the class a story in which a character needs help and asking students to verbalize how the character should ask for help

Remember that these are just suggestions. It is important to carefully consider your own classroom situation. Then, list appropriate application activities for your students on your lesson plan.

Phase 3: Infusion Opportunities
(Generally, the Rest of Week 2)

Infusion opportunities are naturally occurring teachable moments that give students the chance to practice their social skills. Be alert for situations in which students should and do or don't use the **Asking for Help** skill and provide prompts and feedback to reinforce the positive use of the skill and its script. Also be alert for situations in which students use the skill inappropriately and need corrective feedback.

Note that teachable moments occur both in and outside the classroom. For example, students may need to use the **Asking for Help** skill when another student is bullying them, when they are trying to read words that are too difficult for them, when they are doing individual or group work, when they have been sent to the office to pick up something from the school secretary, or when they return to school after an absence and new material has been presented. Indeed, you can ask your students to verbalize the **Asking for Help** skill and script any time that they need to approach an adult or peer for assistance during the school day.

Take some time now to consider your students' classroom and school situations, and then list likely infusion opportunities for your students on your lesson plan.

Social Skills Cue Cards

Following are copies of the cue cards for both versions of the **Asking for Help** skill. The cue cards list the specific steps that you and your students need to follow when using this skill within the Stop & Think process.

Remember, you will find cue cards for all of the core and advanced skills discussed in the manual in Appendix B, along with a number of "Stop & Think Stop Signs" and "Stop & Think Step Signs." Put the cue cards, "Stop Signs" and "Step Signs" in strategic places around your classroom and school and give a cue card booklet to each of your students. All of these aids provide reminders to your students that you want them to make Good Choices so that the Stop & Think process can work well for all of you.

Asking for Help (When Sitting at Your Desk) Skill 4

PreK-1: CORE

 1. **Decide** if you really need to ask for help.

 2. **Raise** your hand and **look** at the person you want help from.

 3. **Wait** until you are recognized.

 4. **Say**, "I need help," in a nice or quiet voice and **tell** the person what you need help with.

The Stop & Think Social Skills Program © 2001 by Sopris West. All rights reserved. To order: 800-547-6747. Code 102CARDPRE.

Asking for Help (When You Need to Approach Someone) Skill 4

PreK-1: CORE

 1. **Walk** up to the person you want help from.

 2. **Look** at the person and **cue** the person to get his or her attention.

 3. **Wait** until you are recognized.

 4. **Say**, "I need help," in a nice or quiet voice and **tell** the person what you need help with.

The Stop & Think Social Skills Program © 2001 by Sopris West. All rights reserved. To order: 800-547-6747. Code 102CARDPRE.

SKILL 5
Waiting for Your Turn

As a teacher, you probably feel like you are always waiting for something—for the morning announcements to be over, for supplies or new textbooks, for your students. Your students also need to wait for things in the classroom—for directions, for others who want to give an answer, for their turn on the computer, and for you! Your students need to learn how to wait for their turn, and they need to practice this skill in different settings, with different people, and under different circumstances. While it would be wonderful if all students automatically knew how to be patient, the reality is that they need to learn and practice the **Waiting for Your Turn** skill.

Phase 1: Teaching
(Generally, Monday, Tuesday, and Wednesday of Week 1)

To teach this skill, first ask your students to **Stop and Think**, and then ask if they **are going to make a Good Choice or a Bad Choice**. Once they have decided to make a Good Choice, begin to teach them the **Waiting for Your Turn** skill.

The **Steps** that students need to follow to learn and demonstrate the **Waiting for Your Turn** skill are:

1. **Get into** the listening position (sitting or standing).
2. **Take** a deep breath and **count** to five.
3. **Say** to yourself, "I know I can wait for my turn."
4. **Listen** to what is being said or **watch** what is happening.
5. **Walk** away and do something else if waiting is too hard.

A shorter, alternative set of steps for the **Waiting for Your Turn** skill is:

1. **Sit** or **stand** in the waiting (listening) position.
2. **Think** about making a Good Choice to wait or think about something else that you're interested in.
3. **Relax** and **watch** for the person you are waiting for to stop, look at you, and ask you what you need.

Part II: Skill Lessons

In situations in which students urgently need you, knowing how to wait patiently will not be enough. In such cases, they also need to know how to interrupt appropriately. The **How to Interrupt** skill is an extension of, and is dependent upon, the **Waiting for Your Turn** skill. In fact, students need to wait patiently two times as part of the **How to Interrupt** skill. Thus, they need to master the **Waiting for Your Turn** skill before they can be successful with the **How to Interrupt** skill. **How to Interrupt** is the next skill covered in this manual. For now, it is best to focus on the **Waiting for Your Turn** skill and helping your students to master it completely.

Once your students are ready to demonstrate **Waiting for Your Turn**, ask them to **Do It!** When your students are successful, have them pat themselves on the back and say, "**Good Job!**"

Remember to teach the **Waiting for Your Turn** skill and every social skill using the same teaching process. This process involves:

1. **Teaching** the steps of the desired social skill

2. **Modeling** the steps and the social skills language (or script)

3. **Role playing** the steps and the language with your students, providing them practice opportunities

4. **Giving performance feedback** to your students as to how accurately they are performing both the script and the new behavior

5. **Applying, and having your students use,** the skill and its steps as much as possible during the day to reinforce the teaching over time, in different settings, with different people, and in different situations

As you initially model, role play, and have your students apply this skill during the day, it is important to choose situations where (1) the skill will be used frequently, (2) the skill will be noticeable—by peers as well as by you and other adults, (3) the skill will be viewed positively, (4) many different people will reinforce your students, and (5) your students are likely to succeed.

Finally, as you plan practice situations for the **Waiting for Your Turn** skill, think about when and where your students already demonstrate this behavior. Also, think about situations where you wish they would demonstrate the behavior.

Suggested Role Plays for This Social Skill

Students have to wait for their turn many times over the course of the school day, and it is a good idea to have them role play a variety of these situations when learning and practicing the **Waiting for Your Turn** skill. The following are some of these situations:

- Waiting for their turn when someone else is called on

- Waiting for their turn when you are helping another student during independent seatwork

- Waiting for their turn when you are giving directions to another student

- Waiting for their turn when playing or talking in an activity center

- Waiting for their turn when you are trying to resolve a conflict involving multiple students

You are encouraged to think about the role-play situations that would be most beneficial for your own students and class. As you do so, feel free to add to or modify this list. Then, jot down your list on your lesson plan for teaching **Waiting for Your Turn**.

Teaching Tips

As your students practice the **Waiting for Your Turn** skill over time, there are a number of things that you can do to help ensure their success.

- First, prompt the **Waiting for Your Turn** skill with a visual cue (e.g., the Stop & Think signal followed by a finger pointing to your wrist or wristwatch) that reminds your students to go through the script and demonstrate the behavior for this skill.

- Second, when you are sure that your students are actively using this skill, give them attention before they get impatient and interrupt inappropriately. Building on success, increase this time period slowly over time.

- Third, make sure that your expectations for waiting are appropriate. For example, preschoolers usually cannot wait patiently for more than 30 seconds, kindergarten students for 60 seconds, and first graders for more than 90 seconds without a special incentive.

- Fourth, verbally reinforce your students when they have successfully used the **Waiting for Your Turn** skill.

Sometimes, especially for younger students, it is appropriate to pair specific incentives or consequences with situations where students have to wait for their turn. For example, when you are going to be working with small groups of students, you may initially want to offer the class bonus points for a special activity (e.g., playing a certain game, using a special program on the computer, or having an afternoon "special treat") as an incentive for successfully using the **Waiting for Your Turn** skill.

When you pair incentives with the use of this skill, you need to choose incentives that are meaningful and desired by your students. You also need to clearly explain the expectations that you have for your students' behavior, the incentive to be earned, and what behavior needs to be demonstrated during the waiting activity in order for the students to earn the incentive. All of this needs to occur before the waiting situation actually occurs.

In addition, it is important to role play the desired behavior with your students so that they are prepared. Then, just before you begin the small-group situation or other situation in which students will need to wait for your help, you should briefly review the Stop & Think steps to **Waiting for Your Turn** and remind your students of the expected behavior and the incentive to be earned.

Over time, if these steps are practiced and implemented correctly, your students should be able to demonstrate the skill more automatically and successfully, and you should be able to fade out the incentive.

If your students are unable to wait appropriately as requested, you will want to use logical or natural consequences. Logical consequences are developed and implemented by you and are logically tied or related to the situation and your students' inability to wait appropriately. Examples of logical consequences might be (1) telling a student that you cannot talk or respond to him or her for a short period of time even after the waiting time is over, (2) withholding the incentive that was promised, and (3) having your students practice the **Waiting for Your Turn** skill for an extra one to three minutes after not performing the skill successfully.

Natural consequences occur normally or naturally as a result of your students' inappropriate behavior. Examples here might include the class period going longer than expected and your students missing a special activity or opportunity that was promised for appropriate behavior, or your continued refusal to attend to a student while he or she is not waiting appropriately for his or her turn.

With either logical or natural consequences, the goal is to motivate students to make a Good Choice the next time. To increase the probability of this happening, be sure to have students practice the

Waiting for Your Turn skill at least three times after a logical or natural consequence occurs.

Phase 2: Application Activities
(Generally, Thursday and Friday of Week 1 and Monday and Tuesday of Week 2)

Remember that the purpose of your application activities is to integrate the social skill that has just been taught into regular, academic, preacademic, or social/interactional lessons. Your goals with application activities are (1) to give your students more opportunities to practice the skill and script as prompted by you, and (2) to give this practice in more real-life classroom, and, perhaps, building situations. The application activities are usually conducted over a 15- to 25-minute period during a regular academic, preacademic, and social/interactional lesson on the three or four days following the teaching of the skill.

Before having your students engage in a classroom-based application activity for **Waiting for Your Turn**, remind them that they will be repeating the steps to the **Waiting for Your Turn** skill and the skill script with you during the activity. Examples of classroom-based tasks or activities in which students can practice the **Waiting for Your Turn** skill and script include the following:

- While waiting in line at the pencil sharpener or water fountain
- While waiting to play with something during free time
- While you are busy helping someone else

Remember that these are just suggestions. It is important to carefully consider your own classroom situation. Then, list appropriate application activities for your students on your lesson plan.

Phase 3: Infusion Opportunities
(Generally, the Rest of Week 2)

Infusion opportunities are naturally occurring teachable moments that give students the chance to practice their social skills. Students need to wait for their turn throughout the school day. Be alert for situations in which students should and do or don't use the **Waiting for Your Turn** skill and provide prompts and feedback to reinforce the positive use of the skill and its script.

Note that teachable moments for **Waiting for Your Turn** occur both in and outside the classroom. For example, students should use this skill when materials are being handed out in class; when they are waiting to enter or leave the classroom or school auditorium; when they are waiting to be dismissed for lunch or from school; and when they are in the cafeteria, at recess, and on field trips.

Take some time now to consider your students' classroom and school situations, and then list likely infusion opportunities for your students on your lesson plan.

Social Skills Cue Cards

The following are copies of the cue cards for the two versions of the **Waiting for Your Turn** skill. These cue cards list the specific steps that you and your students need to follow when using this skill within the Stop & Think process.

Remember, you will find cue cards for all of the core and advanced skills discussed in the manual in *Stop & Think Reproducible Forms*, along with a number of "Stop & Think Stop Signs" and "Stop & Think Step Signs." Put the cue cards, "Stop Signs," and "Step Signs" in strategic places in your classroom and around your school and give each student a cue card. All of these aids provide reminders to your students that you want them to make Good Choices so that the Stop & Think process can work well for all of you.

Waiting for Your Turn Skill 5

PreK-1: **CORE**

 1. **Get into** the listening position.

 2. **Take** a deep breath and **count** to five.

 3. **Say** to yourself, "I know I can wait for my turn."

 4. **Listen** to what is being said or **watch** what is happening.

5. **Walk** away and do something else if waiting is too hard.

The Stop & Think Social Skills Program © 2001 by Sopris West. All rights reserved. To order: 800-547-6747. Code 102CARDPRE.

(A Shorter, Alternative Set of Steps)

Waiting for Your Turn Skill 5

PreK-1: **CORE**

 1. **Sit** or **stand** in the waiting (listening) position.

 2. **Think** about making a Good Choice to wait or think about something else that you're interested in.

 3. **Relax** and **watch** for the person you are waiting for to stop, look at you, and ask you what you need.

The Stop & Think Social Skills Program © 2001 by Sopris West. All rights reserved. To order: 800-547-6747. Code 102CARDPRE.

SKILL 6

How to Interrupt

Your young students are very dependent on you and need your attention. If they need you when you are busy with another task or activity, they need to know how to appropriately interrupt you. They also need to learn when it is appropriate to interrupt you. The **How to Interrupt** skill is an extension of the **Waiting for Your Turn** skill. In fact, students need to use the **Waiting for Your Turn** skill two different times when implementing the **How to Interrupt** skill. Compared to most other skills, your students' success in using the **How to Interrupt** skill will depend on how well you teach the skill and, especially, how you respond to students when using this skill.

Phase 1: Teaching
(Generally, Monday, Tuesday, and Wednesday of Week 1)

To teach this skill, first ask your students to **Stop and Think**, and then ask if they **are going to make a Good Choice or a Bad Choice**. Once they have decided to make a Good Choice, begin to teach them the **How to Interrupt** skill.

The **Steps** that students need to follow for the **How to Interrupt** skill are:

1. **Decide** if you need to interrupt.

2. If you need to interrupt, **walk** up to the person you need.

3. **Make eye contact** with the person, **cue** him or her, and **wait** quietly for your turn.

4. **Say**, "Excuse me" one time to the person you need.

5. **Wait** again until the person stops, looks at you, and asks you what you need.

Once your students are ready to demonstrate the **How to Interrupt** skill, ask them to **Do It!** When your students are successful, have them pat themselves on the back and say, "**Good Job!**"

Remember to teach this and every social skill using the same teaching process. This process involves:

- **Teaching** the steps of the desired social skill

- **Modeling** the steps and the social skills language (or script)

- **Role playing** the steps and the language with your students, providing them practice opportunities

- **Giving performance feedback** to your students as to how accurately they are performing both the script and the new behavior

- **Applying, and having your students use,** the skill and its steps as much as possible during the day to reinforce the teaching over time, in different settings, with different people, and in different situations

As you initially model, role play, and have your students apply this skill during the day, it is important to choose situations where (1) the skill will be used frequently, (2) the skill will be noticeable—by peers as well as by you and other adults, (3) the skill will be viewed positively, (4) many different people will reinforce your students, and (5) your students are likely to succeed.

As you plan practice situations for the **How to Interrupt** skill, think about when and where your students already demonstrate this behavior. Also, think about situations where you wish your students would demonstrate the behavior.

Suggested Role Plays for This Social Skill

Students need to know how to interrupt you, their peers, and other adults and when it is appropriate to do. Thus, it is a good idea to discuss with your students the types of questions or circumstances that are important enough for an interruption. There are an endless number of role-play scenarios for this skill, and it is a good idea to have students role play a variety of them when they are learning and practicing it. The following are some of these situations.

- Interrupting you when you are working one-on-one with another student

- Interrupting you when they need to use the rest room

- Interrupting you or another adult when they are being teased, bullied, or harassed by another student

- Interrupting you when there is an imminent classroom emergency

- Interrupting you when you are speaking with another teacher

- Interrupting a student they are working with when the student is solving a problem the wrong way

- Interrupting an adult on the playground when a fight might begin

You are encouraged to think about the role-play situations that would be most beneficial for your own students and class. As you do so, feel free to add to or modify this list. Then, jot down your list on your lesson plan for teaching the **How to Interrupt** skill.

Teaching Tips

The third step in the **How to Interrupt** skill is the most important step in the process. While students should be fairly good at making eye contact by this time (remember, it is the first step in the **Listening** skill), you will need to teach them how to cue you. That means that you and your students will need to agree upon a specific cue that will indicate that they need to interrupt you. The students could use a "time-out" signal (making a "T" with their two hands), touching their finger to their nose, patting their shoulder with a hand, or anything else. Once established, you will need to practice this cue with your students in the context of the **How to Interrupt** skill. Finally, you will need to demonstrate and practice "waiting quietly" with your students and give them a sense of how long they may have to wait for you under different circumstances (e.g., when you are talking with another student and when you are giving an instructional lesson to a group of students).

You may also want to decide upon a "return" or "response" cue that you can use with your students to indicate that you can't be interrupted right at that moment. The use of this signal will help you by eliminating unnecessary distractions when you don't want to or can't be interrupted, and it will help prevent your students from becoming frustrated because you seem to be taking too long. After deciding on a "return" cue, it is important to role play the "I can't be interrupted" scenario with your students.

Finally, if your students wait and interrupt you correctly and successfully, or if they respond appropriately by walking away when the wait is too long or you have cued that you can't be interrupted, be sure to *very positively* reinforce them for doing a **Good Job!**

Remember that the **How to Interrupt** skill is an extension of the **Waiting for Your Turn** skill. As your students practice these skills over time, there are a number of things that you can do to help ensure their success. Relative to the **Waiting for Your Turn** skill, please review the "Teaching Tips" for that skill for suggestions on how to make this part of the **How to Interrupt** skill successful.

Relative to a separate part of the **How to Interrupt** skill, note that interruptions often occur because students feel that they need your help.

Thus, it is a good idea to review the teaching tips for the **Asking for Help** skill so that you can apply them to this more advanced skill.

Phase 2: Application Activities
(Generally, Thursday and Friday of Week 1 and Monday and Tuesday of Week 2)

Remember that the purpose of your application activities is to integrate the social skill that has just been taught into regular academic, preacademic, or social/interactional lessons. Your goals with application activities are (1) to give your students more opportunities to practice the skill and script as prompted by you, and (2) to give this practice in more real-life classroom and, perhaps, building situations. The application activities are usually conducted over a 15- to 25-minute period during a regular academic, preacademic, or social/interactive lesson on the three or four days following the teaching of the skill.

Before having your students engage in a classroom-based application activity for the **How to Interrupt** skill, remind them that they will be repeating the steps to the skill and the skill script with you during the activity. Examples of classroom-based tasks or activities in which students can practice the **How to Interrupt** skill and script include the following:

- Inform students that you will be meeting/working with them individually at the back of the room and that other students will need to use the **How to Interrupt** skill and script if they need to interrupt you.

- Let students know that you will be grading papers at your desk and that they need to use the **How to Interrupt** skill and script appropriately if they need to interrupt you.

Remember that these are just suggestions. It is important to carefully consider your own classroom situation, then list appropriate application activities for your students on your lesson plan.

Infusion Opportunities (Generally, the Rest of Week 2)

Infusion opportunities are naturally occurring teachable moments that give students the chance to practice their social skills. Students need to use the **How to Interrupt** skill in many settings and with a variety of people when they are at school. Be alert for situations in which students should and do or don't use the **How to Interrupt** skill appropriately and provide prompts and feedback to reinforce the positive use of the skill.

Remember that teachable moments occur throughout the school, not just in the classroom. For example, students should use the **How to Interrupt** skill when they need to get the attention of the school principal or secretary and when they need to interrupt someone in the lunchroom; at recess; or during P.E., music, art, or media classes.

Take some time now to consider your students' classroom and school situations, and then list likely infusion opportunities for your students on your lesson plan.

Social Skills Cue Cards

Below is a copy of the cue card for the **How to Interrupt** skill. This cue card lists the specific steps that you and your students need to follow when using this skill within the Stop & Think process.

Remember, you will find cue cards for all of the core and advanced skills discussed in this manual in *Stop & Think Reproducible Forms*, along with a number of "Stop & Think Stop Signs" and "Stop & Think Step Signs." Put the cue cards, "Stop Signs," and "Step Signs" in strategic places around your classroom and school and give a cue card to each student. All of these aids provide reminders to your students that you want them to make Good Choices so that the Stop & Think process can work well for all of you.

How to Interrupt   Skill 6

PreK-1: **CORE**

 1. **Decide** if you need to interrupt.

 2. If you need to interrupt, **walk** up to the person you need.

 3. **Make eye contact** with the person, **cue** him or her, and **wait** quietly for your turn.

 4. **Say**, "Excuse me" one time to the person you need.

 5. **Wait** again until the person stops, looks at you, and asks you what you need.

The Stop & Think Social Skills Program © 2001 by Sopris West. All rights reserved. To order: 800-547-6747. Code 102CARDPRE.

SKILL 7

Ignoring

Ignoring is a fun skill to teach young students and a valuable skill for them to have. Although you don't want your students to ignore you, they need to know how to ignore distractions, teasing from their peer group, and other students' inappropriate behavior. Thus, you need to teach your students both the skill of **Ignoring** and when to use it.

Phase 1: Teaching
(Generally, Monday, Tuesday, and Wednesday of Week 1)

To teach your students the **Ignoring** skill, first ask them to **Stop and Think**, and then ask if they **are going to make a Good Choice or a Bad Choice**. Once they have decided to make a Good Choice, begin to teach them the **Ignoring** skill.

The following are two different sets of steps for the **Ignoring** skill. The first generic set can be used in almost all situations. The second set (called the "Turtle Technique") is useful when students are sitting down at their desks or working on an activity. With this particular set of steps, you teach your students to ignore by having them literally imitate a turtle.

The **Steps** that students need to follow for the first, more general **Ignoring** skill are:

1. **Look** away, **turn** away, or **walk** away from the person or distraction.

2. **Close** your ears and do not listen.

3. **Be silent**; do not say anything.

The **Steps** that students need to follow for the Turtle Technique are:

1. **Drop** your head like a turtle.

2. **Raise** your shoulders and **put** your hands by your sides.

3. **Focus** on your work or activity.

4. **Be quiet**; don't say anything to the person distracting you.

Once your students are ready to demonstrate the **Ignoring** skill, ask them to **Do It!** When your students are successful, have them pat themselves on the back and say, "**Good Job!**"

Remember to teach **Ignoring** and every social skill using the same teaching process. This process involves:

1. **Teaching** the steps of the desired social skill

2. **Modeling** the steps and the social skills language (or script)

3. **Role playing** the steps and the language with your students, providing them practice opportunities

4. **Giving performance feedback** to your students as to how accurately they are performing both the script and the new behavior

5. **Applying, and having your students use,** the skill and its steps as much as possible during the day to reinforce the teaching over time, in different settings, with different people, and in different situations

As you initially model, role play, and have your students apply this skill during the day, it is important to choose situations where (1) the skill will be used frequently, (2) the skill will be noticeable—by peers as well as by you and other adults, (3) the skill will be viewed positively, (4) many different people will reinforce your students, and (5) your students are likely to succeed.

As you plan practice situations for the **Ignoring** skill, think about when and where your students already demonstrate this behavior. Also, think about situations where you wish your students would demonstrate the behavior.

Suggested Role Plays for This Social Skill

Ignoring is a difficult skill for students of all ages to master. Consequently, role-playing situations in which it is necessary to ignore someone or something is imperative. Some examples of possible role plays follow:

- Ignoring other students when they are displaying inappropriate behavior

- Ignoring a student who is being disruptive in time-out

- Ignoring peers when they are causing distractions during direct instruction

- Ignoring a student who is teasing them

- Ignoring a loud clock or a noise outside

You are encouraged to think about the role-play situations that would be most beneficial for your own students and class. As you do so, feel free to add to or modify this list. Then, jot down your list on your lesson plan for teaching **Ignoring**.

Teaching Tips

You've learned two sets of steps that you can teach for the **Ignoring** skill. Note that if you teach **Ignoring** with the Turtle Technique, you should eventually prompt the skill by simply saying, "Turtle" or "Do the Turtle" to your students. On hearing these words, your students should immediately get into the Turtle position while going through the five Stop & Think steps in their heads. In addition, an important part of your instruction should be teaching your students to recognize when one of their peers is "Doing the Turtle" because of something *they* have done. Seeing a peer in the Turtle position should prompt them to ask themselves if (1) they are bothering one of their seatmates or classmates, (2) they need to **Stop and Think**, and (3) a Good Choice behavior would be to stop bothering the classmate.

Whatever approach you use to teach **Ignoring**, role plays for teaching and practicing the **Ignoring** skill are very important for students at the preschool to early elementary level. You might brainstorm with your students to come up with a list of typical distractions in your class and then set up those situations so that your students can practice **Ignoring** under circumstances that will likely occur in real life. For example, you might have someone tap a student on the shoulder from behind, make background noises in the classroom, tap his or her pencil, or get up too often to throw some paper in the trash.

You might also consider using puppets, dolls, or action figures when you practice the Stop & Think process. Students at the preschool through early elementary school levels learn a great deal through symbolic play. By using puppets or other figures to demonstrate the **Ignoring** skill and then having your students manipulate the puppets to practice the skill, you are providing a wonderful opportunity for modeling, role playing, and performance feedback.

Over time, as your students get better at ignoring different types of distractions during your role plays, you can transfer the skill to real-life situations, prompting and having your students use the skill when distractions actually occur.

Two additional points must be mentioned. First, as noted earlier, students need to understand when and where they should—*and should not*—ignore someone else's behavior. It is critical that you emphasize to your students that they should not use the **Ignoring** skill in situations where their safety may be compromised. In such situations, they should use their **Asking for Help** and **Following Directions** skills, not the **Ignoring** skill. As you choose situations to role play with your students, be sure to include some for which **Ignoring** is not appropriate, so that you can help your students learn when not to ignore.

Finally, as adults, we know that when we ignore someone else's inappropriate behavior, that behavior often increases in frequency and intensity before it eventually decreases and disappears. We often see this when students who want attention or their own way are ignored. Although it is important to help young students understand this principle, they may not have the patience to continue ignoring an escalating distraction until the inappropriate behavior disappears. Thus in these situations, you should teach your students to approach you for help, using the **Asking for Help** skill, if ignoring doesn't work.

Phase 2: Application Activities
(Generally, Thursday and Friday of Week 1 and Monday and Tuesday of Week 2)

Remember that the purpose of your application activities is to integrate the social skill that has just been taught into regular academic, preacademic, or social/interactional lessons. Your goals with application activities are (1) to give your students more opportunities to practice the skill and script as prompted by you, and (2) to give this practice in more real-life classroom and, perhaps, building situations. The application activities are usually conducted over a 15- to 25-minute period during a regular academic, preacademic, or social/interactional lesson on the three or four days following the teaching of the skill.

Before having your students engage in a classroom-based application activity for **Ignoring**, remind them that they will be repeating the steps to the **Ignoring** skill and the skill script with you during the activity. Examples of classroom-based tasks or activities in which students can practice the **Ignoring** skill and script include the following:

- Independent seatwork
- Direct instruction
- Virtually any other learning situation

You might also set up situations where you have students create disruptions so that others can practice the **Ignoring** skill and script. While artificial, these situations provide more real-life classroom opportunities so that students can master this skill more quickly over time.

Remember that these are just suggestions. It is important to carefully consider your own classroom situations. Then, list appropriate application activities for your students on your lesson plan.

Phase 3: Infusion Activities (Generally, the Rest of Week 2)

Infusion activities are naturally occurring teachable moments that give students the opportunity to practice their social skills. Students often need to ignore distractions. Be alert for situations in which students should and do or don't use the **Ignoring** skill and provide prompts and feedback to reinforce the positive use of the skill. Whenever you see your students use the **Ignoring** skill without prompting and when there really is a distraction that they should ignore, be sure to ask the students to repeat with you the Stop & Think script they used. This process will help to reinforce and "infuse" the practice of this skill across time, people, settings, and situations.

Note that teachable moments occur whenever and wherever students need to ignore disruptive or inappropriate behavior. In addition to ignoring distractions in the classroom, students need to use this skill in the hallways, in the cafeteria, at recess, and in many other school settings.

Take some time now to consider your students' classroom and school situations, and then list likely infusion opportunities for your students on your lesson plan.

Social Skills Cue Cards

Below are copies of the cue cards for the two **Ignoring** skills discussed. These cue cards list the specific steps that you and your students need to follow when using these skills within the Stop & Think process.

Remember, you will find cue cards for all of the core and advanced skills discussed in the manual in *Stop & Think Reproducible Forms*, along with a number of "Stop & Think Stop Signs" and "Stop & Think Step Signs." Put the cue cards, "Stop Signs," and "Step Signs" in strategic places around your classroom and school and give a cue card to each student. All of these aids provide reminders to your students that you want them to make Good choices so that the Stop & Think process can work well for all of you.

Ignoring   Skill 7
PreK-1: **CORE**

 1. **Look** away, **turn** away, or **walk** away from the person or distraction.

 2. **Close** your ears and do not listen.

 3. **Be silent**; do not say anything.

The Stop & Think Social Skills Program © 2001 by Sopris West. All rights reserved. To order: 800-547-6747. Code 102CARDPRE.

Ignoring (Using the Turtle Technique)   Skill 7
PreK-1: **CORE**

 1. **Drop** your head like a turtle.

 2. **Raise** your shoulders and **put** your hands by your sides.

 3. **Focus** on your work or activity.

 4. **Be quiet**; don't say anything to the person distracting you.

The Stop & Think Social Skills Program © 2001 by Sopris West. All rights reserved. To order: 800-547-6747. Code 102CARDPRE.

SKILL 8
Dealing With Teasing

Where there are students who interact together, teasing is inevitable. Sometimes, teasing is just good-natured fun, but at other times it occurs because a specific student wants attention. Teasing also can involve put-downs that make other students feel bad about themselves. When hurt or distressed by teasing, students need to know that they can stay in control of the situation, respond to the teasing, and feel good about themselves and their response.

Phase 1: Teaching
(Generally, Monday, Tuesday, and Wednesday of Week 1)

To teach this skill, first ask your students to **Stop and Think**, and then ask if they **are going to make a Good Choice or a Bad Choice**. Once they have decided to make a Good Choice, begin to teach them the **Dealing With Teasing** skill.

The **Steps** that students need to follow for the **Dealing With Teasing** skill are:

1. **Take** a deep breath and **count** to five.

2. **Ignore** the person teasing you, using your **Ignoring** skill.

3. If needed, **say**, "Please STOP IT," in a brave voice.

4. If needed, **walk** away from the person.

5. If needed, **ask** for help, using your **Asking for Help** skill.

Once your students are ready to demonstrate the **Dealing With Teasing** skill, ask them to **Do It!** When your students are successful, have them pat themselves on the back and say, "**Good Job!**"

Remember to teach this and every social skill using the same teaching process. This process involves:

1. **Teaching** the steps of the desired social skill

2. **Modeling** the steps and the social skills language (or script)

3. **Role playing** the steps and the language with your students, providing them practice opportunities

4. **Giving performance feedback** to your students as to how accurately they are performing both the script and the new behavior

5. **Applying, and having your students use,** the skill and its steps as much as possible during the day to reinforce the teaching over time, in different settings, with different people, and in different situations

As you initially model, role play, and have your students use this skill during the day, it is important to choose situations where (1) the skill will be used frequently, (2) the skill will be noticeable—by peers as well as by you and other adults, (3) the skill will be viewed positively, (4) many different people will reinforce your students, and (5) your students are likely to succeed.

As you plan practice situations for the **Dealing With Teasing** skill, think about when and where your students already demonstrate this behavior. Also, think about situations where you wish your students would demonstrate the behavior.

Suggested Role Plays for This Social Skill

Role playing the **Dealing With Teasing** skill should be controlled very carefully. Indeed, each role play should involve only five seconds of teasing. The student who was teased can then demonstrate the **Dealing With Teasing** skill. Limiting the teasing to just five seconds is done to help ensure that the role plays do not hurt any student's feelings or embarrass anyone. For the same reason, the teasing situations modeled in the role plays should focus on characteristics that are either very common to your students or not common at all. The following are some possible situations:

- A student could be teased for writing with his or her left hand (very common)

- A student could be teased for wearing pink-striped pants with little fish on them (highly unlikely scenario)

Note that the practice sessions should also include realistic role plays. For that reason, you are encouraged to ask your students during the initial teaching session if they have ever been teased and, if so, how. If you decide to use any of these situations for role plays, choose only those situations that could involve at least half of the class. Examples might include a student being teased for having a "different" last name, for having to wear a school uniform, or for tripping over some books in class. Be sure to avoid situations that might involve only a few students in the class, such as a student being teased for not knowing his or her letters, since such role plays could cause students to feel embarrassed or hurt.

Take some time now to think about role plays that would be most beneficial to your students and classroom. Then, jot down your list on your lesson plan for teaching **Dealing With Teasing**. You may want to add to your list after receiving student input on actual teasing situations.

Teaching Tips

Dealing With Teasing is the first conflict resolution skill presented in this book. The seven previous skills were survival skills (**Listening, Following Directions,** and **Ignoring**), interpersonal skills (**Using Nice Talk, How to Interrupt,** and **Waiting for Your Turn**), or problem-solving skills (**Asking for Help**). As noted earlier, conflict resolution skills are social skills that help students to deal with significant emotions and emotional situations and to resolve existing interpersonal and intrapersonal conflicts.

Simply put, conflicts occur either externally or internally. That is, they originate either because of external people, events, or situations (interpersonal conflicts) or because of internal perceptions, beliefs, self-statements, or expectations (intrapersonal conflicts). Complicating matters, an external event may create an internal conflict. For example, trying to keep up with a more skilled peer in soccer (an external event) can create an internal conflict if the student *believes* that he or she should be able to play as well as the other student. Since each student has a different belief system, a specific situation may trigger a conflict for one student but not another.

Teasing is considered an external conflict, since the conflict occurs due to external factors. Thus, the **Dealing With Teasing** skill is considered an **external conflict resolution** skill and focuses on teaching or reteaching students to respond (an external action) in appropriate, prosocial ways. In contrast, the other primary conflict resolution skill in this book, **Dealing With Losing**, involves a student's internal reaction to an event and thus is considered an **internal conflict resolution** skill. As will be discussed in more detail in the **Dealing With Losing** skill lesson, the **Dealing With Losing** skill focuses on teaching or reteaching students to *think* (an internal action) in appropriate, prosocial ways and then to link this thinking to appropriate, prosocial behavior.

As a teacher of students at the preschool to early elementary school ages, you need to teach your students how to accurately evaluate teasing situations as well as how to behaviorally respond to teasing. That is, you need to verbalize when it is best to move toward the teasing (e.g., by asking the teaser to stop) and when it is best to move away from the teasing (e.g., by ignoring it, by walking away, or by asking for help). In most cases, students at these age levels should make only one attempt at asking the teaser to stop and then should move away from the teasing if it continues. As students get older and increase their problem-solving and conflict resolution skills, they will become more adept at stopping another person's teasing by directly asking or convincing the person to stop.

Over time and by continually practicing the **Dealing With Teasing** skill, students will learn to evaluate different situations on their own and to identify the best conflict resolution choices. As this occurs, they are increasing both their internal and external self-management skills. For now, though, your students probably are not developmentally ready to do this. It is up to you to help your students with their behavioral responses.

Phase 2: Application Activities
(Generally, Thursday and Friday of Week 1 and Monday and Tuesday of Week 2)

Remember that the purpose of your application activities is to integrate the social skill that has just been taught into regular academic, preacademic, or social/interactional lessons. Your goals with application activities are (1) to give your students more opportunities to practice the skill and script as prompted by you, and (2) to give this practice in more real-life classroom and, perhaps, building situations. The application activities are usually conducted over a 15- to 25-minute period during a regular academic, preacademic, or social/interactional lesson on the three or four days following the teaching of the skill.

Before having your students engage in a classroom-based application activity for **Dealing With Teasing**, remind them that they will be repeating the steps to the **Dealing With Teasing** skill and the skill script with you during the activity.

Since teasing can take place at any time during the day, it is easy to set up situations in which one student teases another student and then to have the student who was teased (and others) practice the **Dealing With Teasing** skill and script. In setting up these practice opportunities, be sure to make it clear to the student who will do the teasing that this is a practice situation and not permission to tease at other times, that you will specify the time when the teasing will occur, you will cue the student to "do" the teasing, the teasing will occur for only five seconds, and you will then oversee (and perhaps guide) the other student's use of the **Dealing With Teasing** skill and script.

It is best to begin with teasing situations that are most common in your classroom and result in little emotional reaction. You can then progress to teasing situations that may result in stronger emotional reactions from the students involved. Examples of situations that you can set up during the school day to provide students with opportunities to practice the **Dealing With Teasing** skill and script include the following:

- Have a student make a "side" comment to a classmate after he or she drops a pencil

- Have a student tease a peer for answering a question incorrectly

- Have a student put down a classmate in front of a group of peers because of the classmate's dress or athletic weakness

Note that the first two situations listed would likely result in less emotional reaction than the last one.

Finally, bear in mind that there are periods during the day when students may be more susceptible to being teased by their peers. These include the beginning of the day before class has started, the time during which buses are being called, and free time. You are encouraged to remind your students to use the **Dealing With Teasing** skill during these times.

Take some time now to carefully consider your own classroom situations. Then, list appropriate application activities for your students on your lesson plan.

Phase 3: Infusion Opportunities (Generally, the Rest of Week 2)

Infusion opportunities are naturally occurring teachable moments that give students the chance to practice their social skills. Students often have to deal with teasing, both in and outside the classroom. Common settings outside the classroom where teasing occurs include the bus loading/discharging area, the playground, the hallways and bathrooms, P.E. and other "special" classes (e.g., music, art, media), and the cafeteria.

Be alert for teasing or potential teasing situations throughout the school day. When a potential teasing situation may or is about to occur, have your students practice the **Dealing With Teasing** skill and script as a way to prevent the teasing or the response to teasing. If the teasing has already occurred, prompt the "offended" party to use the **Dealing With Teasing** skill and script as a Good Choice way to respond.

Take some time now to consider your students' classroom and school situations, and then list likely infusion opportunities for your students on your lesson plan.

Social Skills Cue Cards

Below is a copy of the cue card for the **Dealing With Teasing** skill. This cue card lists the specific steps that you and your students need to follow when using this skill within the Stop & Think process.

Remember, you will find cue cards for all of the core and advanced skills discussed in this manual in *Stop & Think Reproducible Forms*, along with a number of "Stop & Think Stop Signs" and "Stop & Think Step Signs." Put the cue cards, "Stop Signs," and "Step Signs" in strategic places around your classroom and school and give a cue card to each student. All these aids are reminders to your students that you want them to make Good Choices so that the Stop & Think process can work well for all of you.

Dealing With Teasing Skill 8

PreK-1: **CORE**

 1. **Take** a deep breath and **count** to five.

 2. **Ignore** the person teasing you, using your **Ignoring** skill.

 3. If needed, **say**, "Please STOP IT," in a brave voice.

 4. If needed, **walk** away from the person.

 5. If needed, **ask** for help using your **Asking for Help** skill.

The Stop & Think Social Skills Program © 2001 by Sopris West. All rights reserved. To order: 800-547-6747. Code 102CARDPRE.

SKILL 9

Dealing With Losing

Competition is part of the American fabric, and winning is highly valued. Indeed, it is often overemphasized. From sports events to cartoons, games, and toys, students often learn that winning and feeling good about oneself go practically hand in hand.

However, where there is winning there also is losing, and losing is more often associated with failing than with trying. Making matters worse, the feelings of failure that sometimes come from losing may result in anger, depression, frustration, low self-confidence, and withdrawal. For all of these reasons, teachers today need to help their students link competition to learning, growth, skill development, and "trying your best" and to teach them the meaning of losing within that context. They also have to teach their students how to deal with both winning and losing.

In our competitive society, **Dealing With Losing** is a very important skill for young students to learn. And, because the nature of competition changes as students grow older, it is a skill that should be taught at many different age levels.

Phase 1: Teaching
(Generally, Monday, Tuesday, and Wednesday of Week 1)

To teach this skill, first ask your students to **Stop and Think**, and then ask if they **are going to make a Good Choice or a Bad Choice**. Once they have decided to make a Good Choice, begin to teach them the **Dealing With Losing** skill.

The **Steps** that students need to follow for the **Dealing With Losing** skill are:

1. **Take** a deep breath and **count** to five.

2. **Say**, "Everyone can't win every time."

3. **Think** about the last time you won a similar activity and **say**, "Maybe I'll win next time."

4. **Decide** whether you want to play again or do something else.

Once your students are ready to demonstrate **Dealing With Losing**, ask them to **Do It!** When your students are successful, have them pat themselves on the back and say, **"Good Job!"**

Remember to teach this and every social skill using the same teaching process. This process involves:

- **Teaching** the steps of the desired social skill

- **Modeling** the steps and the social skills language (or script)

- **Role playing** the steps and the language with your students, providing them practice opportunities

- **Giving performance feedback** to your students as to how accurately they are performing both the scripts and new behavior

- **Applying, and having your students use,** the skill and its steps as much as possible during the day to reinforce the teaching over time, in different settings, with different people, and in different situations

As you initially model, role play, and have your students use this skill during the day, it is important to choose situations where (1) the skill will be used frequently, (2) the skill will be noticeable—by peers as well as by you and other adults, (3) the skill will be viewed positively, (4) many different people will reinforce your students, and (5) your students are likely to succeed.

As you plan practice situations for the **Dealing With Losing** skill, think about when and where your students already demonstrate this behavior. Also, think about situations where you wish your students would demonstrate the behavior.

Suggested Role Plays for This Social Skill

While competition may not be as prevalent in the preschool/early elementary school years as it is in later years, but your young students still encounter competition and need to know how to prosocially deal with losing. Possible role plays that students at this age level can use to practice the **Dealing With Losing** skill include the following:

- Dealing with losing in an academic activity that involves "teams"

- Dealing with losing when playing a game, such as "Chutes and Ladders," during free time

- Dealing with losing or not being first during the weekly "bonus point" raffle

- Dealing with losing or not coming in first in a game or race during P.E.

- Dealing with not being chosen first when classroom helpers or academic teams are being selected

- Dealing with not being first in other classroom or building academic games, social games, or competitions

You are encouraged to think about the role-play situations that would be most beneficial for your own students and class. As you do so, feel free to add to or modify this list. Then, jot down your list on your lesson plan for teaching **Dealing With Losing**.

Teaching Tips

Like **Dealing With Teasing, Dealing With Losing** is a conflict resolution skill. The main difference between the two skills is that **Dealing With Teasing** involves a conflict with another person (the teaser) and thus is an external conflict resolution skill; whereas, **Dealing With Losing** focuses on a student's perception of an event (i.e., not winning a game) and thus is an internal conflict resolution skill. The internal reactions and emotions that students have as a result of losing are based on their perceptions about what losing is and what losing means. Students who focus heavily on winning and losing rather than on enjoying an activity are in danger of behaviorally "blowing up" when they are in a losing or near-losing situation, especially when they have not learned the **Dealing With Losing** skill.

The **Dealing With Losing** skill focuses on students' cognitive beliefs or self-statements about winning and losing, how those beliefs have been conditioned, and whether they need to be reconditioned so that students can more easily deal with losing in the future. Students who believe that everyone can't win every time or who enjoy doing activities with their classmates without focusing on whether they win or lose probably already possess the beliefs needed to deal with losing in a positive way. However, students who believe, "I must win every time in order to feel good about myself [or for some other reason]" or "It's not fair that everyone else wins and I never win at all" have to be helped to change those beliefs. As a teacher, you can do that by helping those students practice the verbal self-statements in Steps 2 and 3 of the **Dealing With Losing** skill, as well as the behavioral response to losing in Step 4 of the skill, so that they become automatically linked to any win-lose situation.

All of this relates to a critical area of child development and behavior that focuses on the fact that children's internal beliefs and self-statements influence the probabilities of certain behaviors. It's the same for adults. Don't your beliefs about police officers influence how you interact with them when they pull you over on the highway? Don't your beliefs about car salesmen or department store clerks at the returns desk influence your initial behaviors, reactions, and responses toward them? Just as you can recondition your own beliefs, you can recondition your students' beliefs and, therefore, their behaviors. As a teacher of preschool to early elementary students, you also have the exciting opportunity to help shape your students' early belief systems and influence the behaviors that get linked to them.

In teaching and practicing the **Dealing With Losing** skill with your students, it is important to observe your students' reactions to losing or competitive situations and determine what their internal beliefs and self-statements are. Then, you can model and provide feedback on those beliefs and self-statements that are related to winning and losing. By doing so, you can significantly impact how your students will respond to and feel about losing.

As a final note, today's students spend more time in isolated play than ever before. Think about how much time they spend doing video-, computer-, and Internet-based activities. Critically, losing to a computer or video game is different from losing to another person. Losing to a person is an interpersonal, interactional event, whereas losing to a computer is a solitary, one-dimensional event. For most students, losing to a computer results in increased motivation to beat the computer the next time. When students get angry for losing, the game does not respond to their anger or continue the conflict. Ultimately, the student has to decide whether to replay the game or turn it off and walk away.

Losing a game involving other people is different. If a student gets angry for losing, the other people involved can respond to and reciprocate the student's emotional reaction. And, because students today are less involved in interactive, interpersonal play than students in the past, partly due to the amount of time they spend playing computer games and watching TV, they have not learned and/or sufficiently practiced the **Dealing With Losing** skill with other people. The only way to address this situation is to teach your students the **Dealing With Losing** skill, make sure they participate in activities that involve interacting and playing with other students, and model and reinforce the steps of the **Dealing With Losing** skill whenever opportunities present themselves.

Teaching the **Dealing With Losing** skill should not be a one-time event. It should be taught to students early in life and continuously thereafter, because students and the social situations they experience are always changing.

Phase 2: Application Activities
(Generally, Thursday and Friday of Week 1 and Monday and Tuesday of Week 2)

Remember that the purpose of your application activities is to integrate the social skill that has just been taught into regular academic, preacademic, or social/interactional lessons. Your goals with application activities are (1) to give your students more opportunities to practice the skill and script as prompted by you, and (2) to give this practice in more real-life classroom and, perhaps, building situations. The application activities are usually conducted over a 15- to 25-minute period during a regular academic, preacademic, or social/interactional lesson on the three or four days following the teaching of the skill.

Before having your students engage in a classroom-based application activity for **Dealing With Losing**, remind them that they will be repeating the steps to the skill and the skill script with you during the activity. Examples of classroom-based tasks or activities in which students can practice the **Dealing With Losing** skill and script include the following:

- Academic competitions, such as letter or spelling or number or math bees, or academic games in which there will be a winner or a winning team; those who lose should be prompted to practice the **Dealing With Losing** skill and script

- Cooperative group activities set up so that one group will come in first; again, the members of the other teams should be prompted to practice the **Dealing With Losing** skill and script

Whether the activity is a naturally occurring one or one that you set up so that students can practice the **Dealing With Losing** skill, be sure to guide your students through the behavior and script for this skill. You can do this before students start the activity, or after a student or team has won and before anyone makes a Bad Choice as a result of losing. It is also a good idea to issue reminders about using this skill before free or open activity times when students will be playing games that will involve losing.

Take some time now to carefully consider your own classroom situations. Then, list appropriate application activities for your students on your lesson plan.

Phase 3: Infusion Opportunities (Generally, the Rest of Week 2)

Infusion opportunities are naturally occurring teachable moments that give students the chance to practice their social skills. To help your students fully master the **Dealing With Losing** skill and script, be on the alert for situations in which they potentially will need to use the skill (e.g., when they are about to play a game or engage in a competition) or when they have already lost and need to use the skill. Then, have students practice the **Dealing With Losing** skill and script as they prepare for or handle, respectively, the losing situation.

Note that teachable moments for the **Dealing With Losing** skill occur both in and outside the classroom. Thus, it is helpful for adults in settings outside the classroom to be able to reinforce the use of this skill. For example, the P.E. teacher might reinforce the use of the skill both before and after students play team games, and recess monitors might reinforce the use of the skill during games and other situations on the playground.

Take some time now to consider your students' classroom and school situations, and then list likely infusion opportunities for your students on your lesson plan.

Social Skills Cue Cards

Below is a copy of the cue card for the **Dealing With Losing** skill. This cue card lists the specific steps that you and your students need to follow when using this skill within the Stop & Think process.

Remember, you will find cue cards for all of the core and advanced skills discussed in this manual in *Stop & Think Reproducible Forms*, along with a number of "Stop & Think Stop Signs" and "Stop & Think Step Signs." Put the cue cards, "Stop Signs," and "Step Signs" in strategic places around your classroom and school and give a cue card to each student. All these aids are reminders to your students that you want them to make Good Choices so that the Stop & Think process can work well for all of you.

Dealing With Losing

Skill 9

PreK-1: **CORE**

 1. **Take** a deep breath and **count** to five.

 2. **Say**, "Everyone can't win every time."

 3. **Think** about the last time you won a similar activity and **say**, "Maybe I'll win next time."

 4. **Decide** whether you want to play again or do something else.

The Stop & Think Social Skills Program © 2001 by Sopris West. All rights reserved. To order: 800-547-6747. Code 102CARDPRE.

SKILL 10
Accepting Consequences

A major component of the **Accepting Consequences** skill is following directions, for the skill requires students to appropriately follow the directions they receive as a result of making a Bad Choice. For example, if a student does not wait for his or her turn during a game, you might tell the student that he or she has to miss the next turn. Or, if a student responds aggressively to a peer's teasing, you might tell the student to go to time-out. When students follow the directions appropriately, they are demonstrating an important part of the **Accepting Consequences** skill.

The critical difference between the **Accepting Consequences** skill and the **Following Directions** skill is that **Accepting Consequences** is carried out immediately after a student has made a Bad Choice, when his or her emotions might be high. Thus, the first step of the **Accepting Consequences** skill is a self-control/calming-down step. Further, the **Accepting Consequences** skill requires that the student acknowledge and apologize for his or her Bad Choice. And, finally, **Accepting Consequences** requires that the student follow through with the directions of the consequence even though he or she may still be somewhat upset.

Phase 1: Teaching
(Generally, Monday, Tuesday, and Wednesday of Week 1)

To teach this skill, first ask your students to **Stop and Think**, and then ask if they **are going to make a Good Choice or a Bad Choice**. Once they have decided to make a Good Choice, begin to teach them the **Accepting Consequences** skill.

The **Steps** that students need to follow for the **Accepting Consequences** skill are:

1. **Take** a deep breath and **count** to five.

2. **Think** about what is being said.

3. **Say**, "I'm sorry I made a Bad Choice," and specify what should have been done.

4. **Follow** the directions or the steps of the consequence using your **Following Directions** skill.

Once your students are ready to demonstrate the **Accepting Consequences** skill, ask them to **Do It!** When your students are successful, have them pat themselves on the back and say, "**Good Job!**"

Remember to teach this and every social skill using the same teaching process. This process involves:

1. **Teaching** the steps of the desired social skill

2. **Modeling** the steps and the social skills language (or script)

3. **Role playing** the steps and the language with your students, providing them practice opportunities

4. **Giving performance feedback** to your students as to how accurately they are performing both the script and new behavior

5. **Applying, and having your students use,** the skill and its steps as much as possible during the day to reinforce the teaching over time, in different settings, with different people, and in different situations

As you initially model, role play, and have your students use this skill during the day, it is important to choose situations where (1) the skill will need to be used, (2) the skill will be noticeable—by peers as well as by you and other adults, (3) the skill will be viewed positively, (4) many different people will reinforce your students, and (5) your students are likely to succeed.

As you plan the practice situations for the **Accepting Consequences** skill, think about when and where your students already demonstrate this behavior. Also, think about situations where you wish your students would demonstrate the behavior.

Suggested Role Plays for This Social Skill

There are many reasons that students may have to use the **Accepting Consequences** skill in and outside the classroom, and there are many types of consequences they may receive. To help your students practice this skill, have them role play how they should react to a variety of situations. The following are some suggestions:

- Having to go to time-out after behaving inappropriately

- Having to lose a turn in a game because of not playing by the rules

- Having to go to the back of the line because of acting inappropriately when at the front of the line

- Being told that you will be putting their name on the board because of a Bad Choice that they made

- Having to miss recess because of an in-class infraction or because they did not complete a worksheet due to a Bad Choice

You are encouraged to think about the role-play situations that would be most beneficial for your own students and class. As you do so, feel free to add to or modify this list. Then, jot down your list on your lesson plan for teaching **Accepting Consequences**.

Teaching Tips

The following suggestions will help you to teach and reinforce the **Accepting Consequences** skill most effectively.

First, when teaching this skill, it is important to explain to your students that it is okay to make mistakes or to be wrong. You should also emphasize the importance of accepting the consequences and learning from their mistakes so that they can avoid similar mistakes in the future. For example, you might say:

> Sarah, I understand that people sometimes make mistakes or Bad Choices; however, I expect that you will learn from your Bad Choices and make fewer of them in the future. Right now, though, the most important thing to do after you have made a Bad Choice is to admit that you were wrong and to accept the consequence. If you do these two things, I promise that I will not be angry. I may be disappointed in you, but I will not be angry. In general, you know that I want you to make as many Good Choices as you can. That way, I'll always be able to tell you that you did a **Good Job**.

Second, when you practice and use the **Accepting Consequences** skill with your students, remember to use a firm yet matter-of-fact voice. If you use the Stop & Think process with an excessively angry or loud voice, your students might react to the emotionality in your voice and refuse to follow your directions. Then, they may blame you for yelling or getting angry at them, ignore the message that Bad Choices result in bad outcomes, and avoid the fact that they are responsible for their own choices and the resulting consequences. In addition, your students might begin to associate the Stop & Think process with anger and punishment and not with problem solving and learning. Finally, an angry or overly emotional voice will contradict your message that it's all right to make mistakes as long as we learn from them.

Third, recognize that your students will need to be cued or prompted to say, "I'm sorry I made a Bad Choice," and that they sometimes will be imitating you more than actually feeling a high level of remorse. This is especially true for preschool and kindergarten students. Nevertheless, you need to model and reinforce this step in the **Accepting Consequences** skill to help your young students learn to associate remorse and the need to apologize with making a Bad Choice and accepting the consequences. Remorse is a skill that young students need to learn through modeling and experience—it is not innate.

Fourth, remember to praise your students when they successfully use the **Accepting Consequences** skill. Even though you might still be disappointed with your students' prior behavior, it is important to recognize that they are using the **Accepting Consequences** steps and trying to make things better. Praise at this point will reestablish the more positive tone that you want as the situation moves toward resolution.

Finally, after a student has finished his or her consequence, remember to have the student practice the Good Choice behavior that he or she did not demonstrate previously. For example, if a student did not raise his hand and wait for you to call on him when you were asking questions to your class, you might have the student role play the correct way to **Wait for Your Turn**. In fact, it would be helpful to have this student practice the Good Choice behavior two or three times as soon as possible after the consequence is over and things have calmed down. Doing so will help increase the probability that the student will perform the Good Choice behavior in the future.

As you know, the goal of the Stop & Think process is to teach students how to make Good Choices, to encourage or motivate them to make those choices, and to help them understand that they are responsible for their own behavior. Punishment generally doesn't change behavior—providing consequences and opportunities to practice Good Choices changes behavior. That is why it is so important to help your students master the **Accepting Consequences** skill and to have them practice the Good Choice behavior after acting inappropriately.

Phase 2: Application Activities
(Generally, Thursday and Friday of Week 1 and Monday and Tuesday of Week 2)

Remember that the purpose of your application activities is to integrate the social skill that has just been taught into regular academic, preacademic, social/interactional lessons. Your goals with application activities are (1) to give your students more opportunities to practice the skill and script as prompted by you, and (2) to give this practice in more real-life classroom and, perhaps, building situations. The application activities are usually conducted over a 15- to 25-minute period during a regular academic, preacademic, or social/interactional lesson on the three or four days following the teaching of the skill.

Before having your students engage in a classroom-based application activity for **Accepting Consequences**, remind them that they will be repeating the steps to the **Accepting Consequences** skill and the skill script with you during the activity. Examples of classroom-based tasks or activities in which students can practice the **Accepting Consequences** skill include the following:

- Having the class play an academic or social game where students lose points or receive a "penalty" because of errors or Bad Choices; make sure the students practice the **Accepting Consequences** skill and script while responding to their errors or Bad Choices

- Reading the students a story about a boy or girl who makes a Bad Choice and receives a consequence and having students "talk" the child through the **Accepting Consequences** skill.

Take some time now to carefully consider your own classroom situations, then list appropriate application activities for your students on your lesson plan.

Phase 3: Infusion Opportunities (Generally, the Rest of Week 2)

Infusion opportunities are naturally occurring teachable moments that give students the chance to practice their social skills. Students naturally make mistakes or Bad Choices as a function of growing up. Thus, there are many real-life opportunities for you to use and reinforce the **Accepting Consequences** skill. Be alert for situations in which students are likely to make Bad Choices and for teachable moments when the **Accepting Consequences** skill and script can be practiced.

Remember that teachable moments occur throughout the school, not just in the classroom. It is helpful for playground monitors, hallway monitors, and other school staff to be trained in the Stop & Think process and the steps and script for the **Accepting Consequences** skill, since they may be the ones who see Bad Choice behavior and have to implement the consequences.

Take some time now to consider your students' classroom and school situations and then list likely infusion opportunities for your students on your lesson plan.

Social Skills Cue Cards

Below is a copy of the cue card for the **Accepting Consequences** skill. This cue card lists the specific steps that you and your students need to follow when using this skill within the Stop & Think process.

Remember, you will find cue cards for all of the core and advanced skills discussed in this manual in *Stop & Think Reproducible Forms*, along with a number of "Stop & Think Stop Signs" and "Stop & Think Step Signs." Put the cue cards, "Stop Signs," and "Step Signs" in strategic places around your classroom and school and give a cue card to each student. All these aids are reminders to your students that you want them to make Good Choices so that the Stop & Think process can work well for all of you.

Accepting Consequences   Skill 10

PreK-1: **CORE**

 1. **Take** a deep breath and **count** to five.

 2. **Think** about what is being said.

 3. **Say**, "I'm sorry I made a Bad Choice," and specify what should have been done.

 4. **Follow** the directions or the steps of the consequence using your **Following Directions** skill.

The Stop & Think Social Skills Program © 2001 by Sopris West. All rights reserved. To order: 800-547-6747. Code 102CARDPRE.

The Advanced Preschool to Early Elementary School Social Skills

You've now learned the rationale, teaching steps, and implementation process for ten core social skills for preschool to early elementary school students and have likely taught a number of those skills to your students. You've also helped your students transfer the skills to many of the situations that occur in the classroom and school.

In this section, you will learn the skill scripts for ten additional advanced social skills that preschool to early elementary school students often need. These advanced skills are:

- Ignoring Distractions
- Rewarding Yourself
- Sharing
- Deciding What to Do
- Asking for Permission
- Joining an Activity
- Using Brave Talk
- Dealing With Being Left Out
- Dealing With Anger
- Apologizing

The advanced skills are taught by following the same two-week schedule and implementation process that was recommended for teaching the core skills. Thus, after conducting an introductory lesson in which you describe the skill and why it is important, you should begin to teach a skill by asking your students to **Stop and Think** and then asking if they **are going to make a Good Choice or a Bad Choice**. Once your students have decided to make a Good Choice, you can begin to teach them the advanced skill.

When your students are ready to demonstrate a targeted skill, ask them to **Do It!** After they have implemented the skill successfully, have them pat themselves on the back and say, "**Good Job!**"

Be sure to teach these skills using the same teaching process that you used for the core skills. This process involves:

1. **Teaching** the steps of the desired social skill

2. **Modeling** the steps and the social skills language (or script)

3. **Role playing** the steps and the language with your students, providing them practice opportunities

4. **Giving performance feedback** to your students as to how accurately they are performing both the script and the new behavior

5. **Applying, and having your students use,** the skill and its steps as much as possible during the day to reinforce the teaching over time, in different settings, with different people, and in different situations

As you initially model, role play, and have your students apply these advanced skills during the day, it is important to choose situations where (1) the skill will be used frequently, (2) the skill will be noticeable—by peers as well as by you and other adults, (3) the skill will be viewed positively, (4) many different people will reinforce your students, and (5) your students are likely to succeed.

For each skill, you will need to plan appropriate role-play, application, and infusion situations. As you do so, think about when and where your students already demonstrate the behavior. Also, think about situations where you wish your students would demonstrate the behavior.

Scripts for the Advanced Social Skills

The following are recommended scripts for teaching the ten advanced social skills. The social skills cue cards for each of these skills can be found in *Stop & Think Reproducible Forms*.

IGNORING DISTRACTIONS

1. **Look** away or **walk** away from the person or distraction.

2. **Say** to yourself, "I won't look and I won't listen—I'll keep on (working, playing)."

3. Continue to **look** away and focus on your activity.

4. **Say**, "Good Job" to yourself, especially if the distraction continues.

REWARDING YOURSELF

1. **Look** at or **think** about the good thing that you did.

2. **Smile** to and for yourself.

3. **Say** to yourself, "I did a great job of (listening, finishing my work, sharing). Good for me!"

SHARING (OR RESPONDING TO A SHARING REQUEST)

1. **Decide** what you want or have been asked to share.

2. **Look** at the person who wants you to share.

3. **Ask**, "Would you like to play with (this part of my game, activity, etc.) with me?"

4. **Make room** for the person to join you and **give** him or her the thing you have decided to share.

DECIDING WHAT TO DO

1. **Decide** if you are finished with your current activity.

2. **Think** about what you need to do or what you want to do next.

3. **Choose** one activity and **identify** its first step.

4. Get ready to **do** the first step.

ASKING FOR PERMISSION

1. **Think** about what you want or want to do.

2. **Walk** up to the person who needs to give you permission and **look** at him or her.

3. Using your nice voice, **ask** for what you want.

4. **Wait** for the person's response.

JOINING AN ACTIVITY

1. **Walk** up to the person or group that you would like to join.
2. **Look** at the person or group.
3. Using your nice voice, **ask**, "May I play with you (join your activity)?"
4. **Wait** for the response.

USING BRAVE TALK

1. **Decide** whether you need to use brave talk.
2. If you decide that you do need to use brave talk, **walk** up to the person you need to talk to.
3. Use your brave look and **look** directly at the person.
4. Use your brave voice and **say** what you need to say.

DEALING WITH BEING LEFT OUT

1. **Take** deep breaths and **count** to five.
2. **Understand** it's OK to feel: (**sad, upset, frustrated**).
3. **Decide** if you want to ask to be included (with the person or group that has left you out).
4. If not, **think** of something else to do.

DEALING WITH ANGER

1. **Take** a deep breath and **count** to ten.
2. **Think** about the Good Choices you can make. You can:
   a. Tell the person that you are angry and talk about it.
   b. Walk away from the person to a safe place.
   c. Find/ask a teacher or another adult to help you.
3. **Choose** your best choice.

APOLOGIZING

1. **Think** about what you need to apologize for.

2. **Walk** up to the person you need to apologize to.

3. **Look** at the person and **say**, "I'm sorry," explaining why you're sorry or describing what you did wrong.

4. **Listen** to what the person says.

Application Activities

As with the core social skills, you should conduct your application activities to (1) give your students more opportunities to practice the skill and script as prompted by you, and to (2) give this practice in more real-life classroom and, perhaps, building situations. Remember that the purpose of the application activities is to integrate the skill that has just been taught into regular academic, preacademic, or social/interactional lessons. The application activities are usually conducted over a 15- to 25-minute period during a regular academic, preacademic, or social/interactional lesson on the three or four days following the teaching of a skill.

Before having your students engage in a classroom-based application activity for an advanced skill, remind them that they will be repeating the steps to the skill and the skill script with you during the activity. Be sure to set up application activities that are appropriate for your students and classroom.

Infusion Opportunities

Remember that infusion opportunities are naturally occurring teachable moments that give students the chance to practice their social skills. Your students will need to be able to perform each of the advanced skills in a number of different settings and situations. For the remainder of the second week of teaching an advanced skill (and, actually, for the rest of the school year), be alert for situations in which your students should and do or don't use the advanced skills appropriately, and provide prompts and feedback to reinforce their positive use.

As you prepare to teach an advanced skill, you are encouraged to jot down the skill steps, role-play situations, application activities, and infusion opportunities that you plan to use on a lesson plan for that skill.

Other Stop & Think Social Skills

In addition to the ten core and ten advanced social skills covered thus far, there are many other social skills that will benefit your students. You can teach any of these skills following the same schedule and implementation process as for the previous skills. However, you will need to identify the specific skill steps and script. To do so, simply think about what your students need to do to implement the skill. Remember to use as few steps as possible and to use language that is easy to understand. Once you have done that, you will be ready to teach the skill using the Stop & Think language and process. Although the following is not an exhaustive list, here are some additional skills you may want to teach your students:

Saying Thank You

Paying Attention to Tasks

Completing Assignments

Offering Help to an Adult

Asking a Question

Making Corrections

Being Prepared to Work

Introducing Yourself

Giving Instructions

Playing a Game

Asking a Favor

Offering Help to a Classmate

Gathering Information

Concentrating on a Task

Suggesting an Activity

Returning What You Borrow

Keeping Promises

Moving Around the Classroom

Using "I" Messages

Knowing Your Feelings

Expressing Your Feelings

Recognizing Another's Feelings

Dealing With Contradictory Messages

Expressing Concern for Another

Expressing Affection

Standing Up for Your Rights

Standing Up for a Friend

Responding to Persuasion

Being Able to Say No

Using Self-Control

Knowing What Your Abilities Are

Arranging Problems by Importance

Doing Your Share

Staying Out of Fights

Problem Solving

Negotiating

Getting Ready for a Difficult Conversation

Having Clear Expectations

Dealing With Boredom

Deciding What Caused a Problem

Making a Complaint

Answering a Complaint

Convincing Others

Showing Sportsmanship

Knowing Your Own Strengths

Dealing With Embarrassment

Accepting No

Relaxing

Talking About Feelings

Understanding the Teacher's Moods

Dealing With Wanting Something That Isn't Yours

Making a Decision

Following the Leader

Being a Good Leader

Sharing Friends

Being Patient With Others

Being Honest

Being Interested in Others

Helping Someone With a Problem

Telling Someone When a Friend Needs Help

Being Organized

Other: _____

Other: _____

Other: _____

Other: _____

Other: _____

Other: _____

Classroom and Building Routines

At the beginning of every school year, students need to learn a number of basic classroom and school-building routines. Just like the social skills already discussed, these routines can be effectively taught using the Stop & Think process.

When teaching these routines, remember to begin by asking your students to **Stop and Think**, and then asking them if they **are going to make a Good Choice**. (Note how these routines allow for only Good Choices.) Once your students have decided to make a Good Choice, you can begin to teach them the targeted routine. When your students are ready to demonstrate the routine, ask them to **Do It!**, and when they have successfully demonstrated the routine, have them pat themselves on the back and tell themselves that they've done a **Good Job!**

As when teaching social skills, you should use the following steps when teaching building and classroom routines:

1. **Teaching** the steps of the desired routine

2. **Modeling** the steps and the Stop & Think language (or script)

3. **Role playing** the steps and the language with your students, providing them practice opportunities

4. **Giving performance feedback** to your students as to how they are doing with both the language and the new behavior

5. **Applying, and having your students use,** the routine and its steps as much as possible during the day to reinforce the teaching over time, in different settings, with different people, and in different situations

The steps for a number of classroom and school-building routines follow. Naturally, you can add to or modify the routines listed here given your expectations and the age level of your students. The most critical thing to remember is that you need to teach these routines to your students and then to provide them with opportunities to practice the expected behaviors while verbalizing the skills within the Stop & Think scripts. If you and they *practice* these behaviors and skills consistently—especially during the first three weeks of school, your students should more automatically and independently demonstrate these skills for the remainder of the school year.

Classroom Routines

ANSWERING QUESTIONS DURING LESSONS

1. **Think** of the answer to the question.
2. **Raise** your hand and **close** your mouth.
3. **Show Listening** and **wait** to be called on.
4. After being called on, **answer** the question.

CONTRIBUTING TO DISCUSSIONS

1. **Decide** what you want to say.
2. **Make sure** it is appropriate to the discussion.
3. **Raise** your hand and **close** your mouth.
4. **Stay** in the Listening Position and **wait** to be called on.
5. **Say** what you want to say.

DOING SEATWORK ASSIGNMENTS

1. **Name**—Put your name on the paper.
2. **Directions**—Read the directions with the teacher.
3. **Problem**—Answer the first problem or question.
4. **Review**—Check your work and go on to the next problem.

WHAT TO DO AFTER COMPLETING A CLASSROOM ASSIGNMENT

1. **Check** your name and heading.
2. **Look over** your work.
3. **Put** your assignment in a safe or designated place.
4. **Decide** what to do next or **wait** for your teacher's directions.

TRANSITIONS FROM ONE CLASSROOM SUBJECT TO ANOTHER

1. **Listen** to your teacher's "Three-Minute Warning."
2. **Finish** up your work.
3. **Put** your work away when your teacher tells you to.
4. **Take out** the next work when your teacher tells you to.
5. **Look** at your teacher and **wait** for the next direction.

BRINGING MATERIALS TO CLASS

1. **Think** about the materials you need for class.
2. **Collect** the materials and put them in a safe place.
3. **Make sure** you have everything.
4. **Take** your materials with you into class.

ENTERING A CLASSROOM

1. **Open** the door and **walk** in quietly. (Or, **wait** for your teacher's direction if you are with him or her.)
2. **Close** the door and **think** about where you are going.
3. Quietly **walk** to that place.
4. **Begin** your next activity or **wait** for your teacher's direction.

HANGING COATS AND BACKPACKS

1. **Walk** to the coat/backpack area.
2. **Hang** up your items where they belong.
3. **Walk** to your seat and **sit** down.
4. **Look** at the board or your folder and quietly **begin** your morning seatwork.

TAKING A TIME-OUT

1. **Take** a deep breath and **count** to five.
2. **Walk** to the time-out chair.
3. **Sit** down, **relax**, and **be quiet**.
4. **Think** about making a Good Choice.

WHEN THE TEACHER IS ABSENT

1. **Use** your **Entering the Classroom** skill.
2. **Hang** up your items where they belong.
3. **Walk** to your seat and sit down.
4. **Look** at the board or your folder and quietly **begin** your morning seatwork.
5. **Listen** to your substitute teacher and **follow** all of his or her directions.
6. **Treat** your substitute teacher just like your regular teacher.

VISITORS IN THE CLASS OR BUILDING

1. **Stay** in your area.
2. **Be quiet**, show a happy smile.
3. **Focus** on your work.
4. **Greet** the visitor if your teacher asks you to.
5. **Answer** any questions politely.

LINING UP TO LEAVE A CLASSROOM (DURING THE SCHOOL DAY)

1. **Stand** up and **put** your chair under your desk.
2. **Walk** to the door of the classroom and **move** into the line.
3. Keep your **eyes** forward in the line, **hands** by your sides, **mouth** quiet, and **space** yourself away from the person in front of you.
4. **Wait** for your teacher's direction to leave.

Building Routines

DISMISSAL

1. **Get ready** to be dismissed: All books/materials in your backpack, coat on, backpack on your back.

2. **Stand** up and **put** your chair under your desk.

3. **Wait** for the bell and your teacher's dismissal.

4. **Walk** to the door and **get** in line.

WALKING IN LINE IN THE BUILDING

1. Keep your **eyes** on the line leader (pilot).

2. **Walk** in the line, **keep** your distance from the student in front of you.

3. Keep your **hands** by your sides.

4. Keep your **voice** quiet.

5. Keep your **feet** quiet but moving.

BATHROOM BEHAVIOR

1. **Go** into the bathroom silently.

2. **Take** your turn.

3. **Flush** when done.

4. **Wash** your hands—one person at the sink at a time.

5. **Dry** your hands with one paper towel and **put** it in the wastebasket.

6. **Walk** out and **get** into line.

GETTING FOOD IN THE CAFETERIA

1. **Show** good line behavior.
2. **Get** your tray and silverware.
3. Keep your **hands** to yourself.
4. **Use** your inside voice.
5. **Take** your food when it is offered.
6. **Say**, "Thank you."

BUSING FOOD/TABLES IN THE CAFETERIA

1. **Stand** up.
2. **Check** to see what needs to be cleaned in your area.
3. **Pick up** any things on the table or floor that need to be taken care of.
4. **Walk** to the busing area.
5. **Put** everything in its proper place (recycling, trash, silverware, and tray busing areas, etc.).
6. **Walk** to your dismissal line.

ENTERING THE AUDITORIUM

1. Keep your **mouth** closed.
2. **Walk** to the front/empty seats first.
3. **Get** into the listening position.
4. **Wait** patiently for the program to begin.

AUDIENCE BEHAVIOR

1. **Be quiet.**
2. **Listen** to the speaker.
3. **Stay** in the listening position.
4. **Clap** at the end of the program.

PLAYING GAMES AT RECESS

1. As a group, **set** the rules and **decide** who goes first.
2. Make sure **everybody** takes a turn.
3. **Compliment** one another—be a good winner and loser.

DECIDING WHETHER TO FOLLOW THE GROUP

1. **Decide** if the group is making a Good Choice or a Bad Choice.
2. If it is making a Bad Choice, **refuse** to also make the Bad Choice.
3. **Tell** the group what you feel or think.
4. **Walk** away for now.

WHEN TO ASK AN ADULT FOR HELP

1. If there is a problem, danger, or someone might get hurt:
2. **Walk** to the nearest adult and get his or her attention.
3. **Tell** the adult exactly what is happening in a calm voice.

WALKING AWAY FROM A FIGHT/CONFLICT

1. **Break eye contact.**
2. **Say** nothing or **say**, "I'm going to walk away for now—we can try to solve this situation later."
3. **Turn** and **walk** away for now.

or

1. **Break eye contact.**
2. **Drop** your arms and shoulders (your body posture).
3. **Say** nothing or **say**, "I'm going to walk away for now—we can try to solve this situation later."
4. **Back away.**

RESPONDING TO THE SAFETY PATROL

1. **Stop** and **listen** politely.
2. **Follow** the directions provided.
3. **Find** an adult if you disagree with the safety patrol; **do not argue**.

GETTING ON THE BUS

1. **Line up** quietly.
2. **Walk** to the back of the bus.
3. **Sit** three to a seat, facing forward.
4. **Put** books/backpack on your lap.

RIDING ON THE BUS

1. **Sit** down, facing forward.
2. Keep your **hands** on your lap.
3. Keep your **feet** in front of you or on the floor.
4. **Use** an inside voice.

Part III

Making the Stop & Think Process Work Most Effectively

Talking With Students

Throughout this manual, suggestions have been made about good ways to talk with your students when using the Stop & Think process. The following are eight important reminders. By following these suggestions, you will help create a positive and proactive environment that will greatly support the teaching and learning process in your classroom.

Reminder 1: Listen to your students with your full attention.

Remember, the first Stop & Think skill is **Listening**, and the second Stop & Think teaching step is **Modeling**. If you are not modeling listening with your full attention when your students are talking with you, then you really cannot expect your students to learn or demonstrate the same skill for you.

Reminder 2: Acknowledge your students' feelings and help your students learn to label them.

Preschool to early elementary school students are just beginning to learn about different emotions and how to handle them. When you label your students' emotions while using the Stop & Think process to teach them social skills, you are helping them to distinguish between different feelings and emotions and to connect those emotions to specific Stop & Think skills. Clearly, if a student labels most of his or her feelings as "anger," then he or she will think and respond in an angry way across many situations and emotions. If you teach your students to distinguish between anger, frustration, fear, failure, and disappointment, for example, then they will understand and respond to a wide range of feelings.

In addition, it is important to acknowledge your students' feelings. If a student says that he or she is angry about something or someone, it is not helpful to deny or discourage the student's feelings by saying, "No, you're not angry," or "You should not be angry about that." *Everyone* has emotions. If students are taught to deny or internalize their emotions, they will not learn how to express those emotions appropriately or how to cope with or respond to them effectively. By acknowledging your students' feelings, you can connect them to the Stop & Think process and teach them how to control their emotions so that Bad Choices don't result.

Part III: Skill Lessons

Reminder 3: Talk with your students using a problem-solving approach, help your students to problem solve, and teach your students the problem-solving process.

When you talk with your students, especially during conflict situations that you are having with them, model and use the Stop & Think process. Describe the problem that you are having and tell your students that you all need to **Stop and Think**. Then analyze the situation together and decide what Good Choice solutions are available and what Bad Choice options are possible. Help your students to think about the positive outcomes resulting from Good Choices and the consequences of Bad Choices. Be open to the fact that your students may come up with some very good solutions. After identifying the best Good Choice solution, talk about the steps needed for implementation and how long these steps will take. Then, **Do It!**

By problem solving difficult situations with your students over time, you will decrease the number of times that you demand or order them to do things. And, as a result, you will decrease their resistance to your authority, increase their motivation and commitment to the choices made, and help them to become independent problem solvers. You will also increase the number of times that you can tell yourself that you did a **Good Job!** as you become an even more successful teacher!

Reminder 4: Don't forget the power of nonverbal and one-word signals that represent entire Stop & Think skills.

Remember to pair the Stop & Think skills and skill steps with nonverbal and one-word signals so that you don't have to go through an entire Stop & Think script each time it is used. For example, the calming down step of the **Dealing With Anger** skill could be paired with a clenched fist (to represent anger) followed by an open palm (to symbolically represent the need to relax). In addition, you might use the one-word signal "relax" to communicate the same thing. Remember that the Stop & Think process is all about conditioning students to respond to situations with an immediate Good Choice response by using their internal language. Pairing the Stop & Think skills and/or steps with a nonverbal or one-word signal actually strengthens this process, helping students' responses become more automatic.

Reminder 5: Use the Stop & Think process with an appropriate volume and tone of voice.

As noted earlier, if you use the Stop & Think process with an excessively angry or loud voice, your students then might react to the emotion in your voice and refuse to follow your directions. Then, they may blame you for yelling and getting angry at them, ignore the message that Bad Choices result in bad outcomes, and avoid the fact that they are responsible for their own choices and the resulting consequences. In addition, your students might associate the Stop & Think process with anger and punishment instead of with problem solving and learning. Finally, an angry or overly emotional voice will contradict the first step of the Stop & Think process, a step that is intended to help your students calm down enough to successfully perform the rest of the skill.

Reminder 6: Give students time—Be patient, don't talk too much, and give your students a chance to work things out on their own.

As your students demonstrate needs that can be linked to the Stop & Think process, guide them using the Stop & Think language and skills. When they approach you with a problem, give them a Stop & Think prompt, and then watch them use the process. Over time, they need to learn to (1) make choices, (2) **Do It!**, (3) make mistakes, (4) practice and learn to mastery, and (5) transfer and apply their training and learning. They need to experience the satisfaction of making Good Choices or, if they are unsuccessful, the logical or natural consequences of making Bad Choices. Remember that Bad Choices and consequences are sometimes necessary if students need to learn from them. Consequences can help students decrease the number of Bad Choices and increase the number of Good Choices that they make over time. By giving your students the opportunity to experience the entire Stop & Think process from beginning to end, you will help them to become more independent and better self-managers.

Reminder 7: Reinforce your students for making Good Choices, prompt their self-reinforcement, and reinforce their independent self-reinforcement.

From preschool to the late elementary school level, students increase their developmental readiness to reinforce themselves, to depend on their own feedback (as fewer adults are around to provide reinforcement), and to reinforce themselves when they make Good Choices that are not seen or acknowledged by anyone else. When you reinforce your students, do it positively, specifically, and unconditionally (remember the 5-to-1 Rule). Be careful to not give a back-handed compliment, in which you positively reinforce your students and then ask why they couldn't make the same Good Choice earlier.

Similarly, it is important to prompt your students to reinforce themselves for doing a good job. A comment as simple as, "Tell yourself you did a Good Job and give yourself a pat on the back" will help your students learn to consistently practice self-reinforcement.

Finally, as you see your students reinforcing themselves for doing a Good Job, be sure to reinforce them for making these statements. Self-reinforcement is an important component of positive self-esteem. It becomes increasingly important as your students head toward adolescence and greater autonomy.

Reminder 8: Give your students hope. Give them reason to expect success and improvement. Give them opportunities to see situations differently. Give them a chance to see themselves more positively and as being valued.

Grade-Level and Building-Level Teams

While it is vital that the social skills in the Stop & Think process be taught in the classroom by individual teachers, the ideal situation is for every social skill to be planned, taught, and reinforced in basically the same way by every teacher at each specific grade level. Schools that carry out this process building-wide are referred to as **Stop & Think** schools. In such schools, every Grade 1 or Grade 3 or Grade 6 teacher (and other school personnel, as described later in this section) teaches the social skills for that grade level using the same skill steps and basically the same skill scripts. That is, while the scripts may differ between grades, they will be the same within each specific grade.

To facilitate the planning and implementation of such social skills training, it is recommended that grade-level teams made up of at least three teachers meet on a monthly basis to discuss the Stop & Think curriculum. (Schools with fewer than three teachers at a grade level may want to use cluster-level teams instead. Cluster-level teams involve personnel from clusters of grade levels—typically, PreK to Grade 1, Grade 2 to Grade 3, and Grade 4 to Grade 5 or 6.) As described in the following sections, it is recommended that each grade-level or cluster-level team have a **social skills team leader** and that these team leaders form the core of a building-level **School Climate** or **School Discipline and Safety Team**.

The Role of Social Skills Team Leaders

Social skills team leaders should be selected before individual teachers formally begin to teach the Stop & Think social skills in their classrooms. These team leaders will help to oversee the social skills process in the building by guiding and monitoring the implementation of the process within their grade levels and by linking grade-level social skills instruction to what is happening in the entire building relative to social skills implementation and student discipline and behavior.

More specifically, social skills team leaders should engage in the following activities:

1. Generate enthusiasm among colleagues and students and provide them with support and encouragement to help maintain a high level of social skills implementation and success in the classroom.

2. Help to identify and validate the teaching steps for each social skill to be taught during a particular month and give a copy of the finalized steps for those skills to the principal prior to the beginning of the month.

3. Model social skills teaching, application, and/or infusion activities in the classroom for other grade-level teachers or team members.

4. Track the implementation and success of classroom-based social skills instruction and monitor student discipline problems or issues that may be or become building-level problems.

5. Help their colleagues (and/or other building staff) to identify the advanced social skills that they want or need students to work on, and help them to agree on the teaching steps for these new skills so that the entire grade level is teaching, discussing, and implementing these skills in the same way.

6. Serve as a communication link between the grade level and the building-based School Climate or School Discipline and Safety Team.

To accomplish virtually all of these activities, the social skills team leader for each grade level should convene a grade-level meeting to be attended by all members of the grade-level team toward the end of each month to:

1. **Debrief** the social skills that were taught the previous month; how the specific skill steps chosen by the grade level worked; and how the teaching, application, and infusion activities were received.

2. **Prebrief** the social skills planned for the next month, deciding if the students are ready to move on to one or two new social skills, agreeing on what those one or two skills will be, determining what the specific skill steps for each chosen skill will be, and specifying exactly when the skills will be taught.

3. **Collect** lists of new social skills role plays used by teachers in the grade level during the previous month to help students practice that month's selected social skills.

4. **Collect** lists of social skill application activities used by teachers in their classrooms to help their students practice the previous month's selected social skills.

5. **Review** the number of times and how the previous month's selected social skills were reinforced in the classroom (and elsewhere) as part of the infusion process.

All of this information should be documented so that a running record is kept that tracks the implementation of the Stop & Think process. It is helpful to use a meeting report form such the one included at the end of this section for this purpose; one can be found in *Stop & Think Reproducible Forms*. Some type of meeting report is strongly recommended so that grade-level teams are accountable both to the Stop & Think process and to themselves and so that decisions and approaches that work are carried on from year to year and don't need to be reinvented.

The Role of the Building-Level School Climate or School Discipline and Safety Team

In schools implementing the Stop & Think social skills process on a buildingwide level, it is recommended that a building-level School Climate or School Discipline and Safety Team be formed to facilitate the ongoing social skills implementation and evaluation process. The grade-level social skills team leaders should form the core of this team. Other team members should include the building principal and representatives of (1) the special education and curricular support (e.g., Title I, reading/math support) teachers; (2) the "special arts" and enrichment teachers (e.g., music, art, P.E., media); (3) the pupil personnel specialists (e.g., the school psychologist, social workers, and/or counselor educators); (4) the classroom paraprofessionals and teacher assistants; and (5) the building's support network (e.g., secretaries, cafeteria workers, custodians, and/or bus drivers).

Once constituted, this team should meet monthly and do the following things:

1. Collect the lists of social skills to be taught at each grade level during the following month, input the lists onto a monthly master calendar, and give the calendar to all of the personnel who will or may be teaching the skills.

2. Discuss how the social skills are working at the grade levels and across the building.

3. Discuss ways for staff and students to continue using the Stop & Think social skills language on a daily basis across the building.

4. Identify the existence of any building-level "special situations" that require attention, conduct the needed analyses of these situations, and plan and implement interventions. Special situations are defined as buildingwide behavioral situations involving problems that occur in a school's more public areas and

that involve students but are not completely caused by or solved through interventions only with these students. Often, special situations involve problems in such places as the school's cafeteria, hallways, buses, playgrounds, and media centers.

In addition, over time the team should:

1. Help to develop, implement, and periodically review the classroom-level, grade-level, and buildingwide accountability system that identifies expected student behavior (with corresponding incentives) and different levels of inappropriate student behavior (with corresponding consequences).

2. Help to create a climate that facilitates staff comfort and competence with the social skills and that encourages and reinforces the consistent use of the social skills and accountability systems developed.

3. Monitor the data management system for tracking the outcomes and success of the program at student, teacher, grade, and building levels. Based on the data collected, the team can then plan or recommend such activities as buildingwide celebrations for staff and students who have made continuous Good Choices.

4. Determine the need for additional social skills, time-out, or behavioral intervention training for the school staff.

5. Track the use of the Stop & Think process by secretaries, aides, cafeteria workers, custodians, and so forth; determine the need for "booster training" with these groups; and determine ways to continue encouraging their appropriate use of the Stop & Think language and process.

6. Begin to develop building-level prevention, intervention, and crisis response plans and processes.

7. Involve students, parents, community agencies and programs, and other community leaders in a collaborative effort that supports all of these goals and that extends the social skills training and implementation to students' homes and the community.

Implementing a Year-Long Social Skills Calendar

With all of the skills presented in this manual, as well as the classroom and building routines and other skills that you add, how should you determine how many skills to teach over the school year, which they should be, and when they should be taught?

With regard to the first issue, in a 36-week school year, you will generally have approximately 30 weeks during which you can teach skills. Not counted here are weeks near school vacations, weeks used for proficiency and national norm-referenced testing, weeks that include staff release/professional development days, and weeks including student field trips. Since each skill is taught over a two-week period, no more than 15 skills can realistically be taught during any school year. And generally, the maximum number at the preschool to early elementary school level is ten, since most students at this level simply cannot handle learning, remembering, and demonstrating any more than ten skills.

With regard to which skills should be taught and when, the order in which skills are presented in this manual represents an order that many teachers have found successful. That is, it is recommended that the core skills be taught first, in the order presented, followed by several of the advanced or other skills if time permits. However, four points must be stressed.

First, this sequence of skills is recommended but is *not* required. What *is* required is that grade-level teams (in Stop & Think schools) and individual teachers (in schools in which the skills are not being taught schoolwide) decide (1) how many and what skills will be taught over the school year, (2) the sequence in which these skills should be taught, and (3) the skill steps and scripts that will be used. Note that these decisions will likely differ from grade level to grade level. Most schools, however, teach the same first four or five social skills to each grade level (i.e., **Listening, Following Directions, Asking for Help**), using age-appropriate steps and practice opportunities, at the same time at the beginning of the school year.

Second, although the ten core skills are generally taught first, grade-level teams or individual teachers (again, in schools where the social skills are not being taught schoolwide) may decide to substitute one or more of the advanced skills or other skills for some of the core skills. The students in a specific grade level might, for example, already be skilled in some of the core skills and ready to learn the advanced skills. Or, the students in

Part III: Skill Lessons

a specific grade level may be experiencing social skill or behavioral difficulties that need to be immediately addressed by the teaching and practice of a social skill that wasn't in the original sequence. It is important to individualize and flex your social skills instruction to the proficiency level and immediate behavioral needs of your students, just as you flex your teaching of academic skills within the context of your year-long academic program.

Third, grade-level teams or individual teachers may choose to teach fewer than ten to 15 social skills. Generally, this occurs because the teacher, the students, or both are becoming overwhelmed with either the number of social skills being presented or the pace of the instructional process. However, it is important that social skills be taught frequently enough to reinforce the importance of the *Stop & Think Social Skills Program* and help ensure that students begin to transfer and independently use the skills in the classroom and school building. Thus, if you are teaching fewer than ten skills, you should integrate a number of "reinforcement weeks" into the schedule, where you explicitly review two or three previously taught social skills with your students. During these weeks, give your students additional practice, application activities, and infusion opportunities with the selected skills, so that their use of the skills becomes more automatic and evident across settings and situations.

Fourth, even though you or your grade-level team will develop a calendar specifying a particular list of skills, bear in mind that once your students have learned the Stop & Think language, the process can be used for any situation that comes up where a specific skill has not yet been taught. Here, all that you need to do is prompt your students to **Stop and Think** and to decide whether they **are going to make a Good Choice or a Bad Choice**. Then, you can use the **What are your Choices or Steps** question to guide or prompt your students to develop the procedures needed to solve the problem at hand or to demonstrate the social skill needed.

Thus, the order of the skills presented in this manual is meant to serve as a guide to the implementation of the Stop & Think process and not as a "must be followed" schedule. It is important to remain flexible and to strategically arrange the skills you teach according to the needs of your students and grade level.

Facilitating the Transfer of Training

As you know, the ultimate goal of the Stop & Think social skills process is to teach students to respond to social and interpersonal situations in positive, proactive, and Good Choice ways. To help ensure that students' use of Good Choice behaviors will become automatic and natural and will occur in a variety of situations, the *Stop & Think Social Skills Program* incorporates a transfer of training process. That is, instruction moves from formal skill lessons to three or four "application days," in which students practice the skill as part of already-existing academic or classroom lessons, to three or four "infusion days," in which the use of the skill is reinforced throughout the school during teachable moments.

These teaching, application, and infusion activities will go a long way in facilitating the transfer of social skills training. However, other activities are also necessary and helpful. Given that the transfer of training involves students' use of Stop & Think social skills across time, settings, people, and situations, the following activities are recommended.

Facilitating Transfer Across Time

During the school year, be sure to use the social skills (and scripts) that have been taught as much as possible during the day. In addition to focusing on the skill that you are currently teaching, watch for teachable moments during which you can provide practice in previously taught social skills (and social skills scripts as needed) and during which you can reinforce your students for using the scripts and demonstrating the appropriate behavior. Indeed, not just classroom teachers but everyone in the building (teachers, administrators, students, custodians, paraprofessionals, and so forth) should be reinforcing the use of social skills at all times.

The most influential factor in facilitating the transfer of training across time is the use of the Stop & Think language. Anyone walking through a Stop & Think school should hear one or more of the five Stop & Think steps at least once every five minutes. That is, students and staff throughout the building should be continually using the Stop & Think language to practice skill scripts, to apply the skills and scripts in real-life situations, and to reinforce their successful use.

Facilitating Transfer Across Settings

The easiest way to ensure that social skills are transferred across settings is to post visual and other Stop & Think reminders throughout the school. Stop & Think signs need to be everywhere in the building; and staff, students, and others should be using the Stop & Think language (or one or two parts of it) at every opportunity. Creating a Stop & Think environment will increase the probability that Stop & Think behavior will occur, especially with students who have been "conditioned" to the Stop & Think language, skills, and process.

In addition, it is helpful for you (and other teachers) to teach Stop & Think skills in different settings across the school, especially when you see that they are needed in those different places. For example, while you may initially teach the **Listening** or **Following Directions** skill in your classroom, you may find that you need to reteach it on the playground or in music, art, P.E., or the cafeteria. Students may not understand that specific social skills must be used in settings outside of their classrooms until a social skill lesson is actually conducted in those other settings.

Finally, in Stop & Think schools, someone at the building level (e.g., the principal or assistant principal, the school psychologist or counselor, the lead teacher or consulting teacher) should be informed about the social skills and skill steps that each grade level will teach the following month so that he or she can put this information on a monthly master calendar and distribute it to everyone in the building. It is especially important that music, art, P.E., media, and other teachers who see students from multiple grade levels receive the calendar. With the information about skills and skill steps being taught at each grade level, these individuals can help reinforce the social skills for each new month with the correct social skills scripts, thereby facilitating the transfer of these skills across settings.

Facilitating Transfer Across People

As noted earlier, the ideal situation is for everyone in the building to be using the Stop & Think language and reinforcing student use of the social skills. It is also important that people other than classroom teachers be able to conduct Stop & Think social skills lessons when necessary. If, for example, students in a music class are making Bad Choices, the music teacher may have to postpone a music lesson and teach a social skills lesson instead. By doing so, the music teacher will emphasize to the students that (1) he or she has as much command of the social skills process as their classroom teacher; (2) the Stop & Think process will be used in music, as well as in all other classes across the school; (3) the students will be held accountable for their behavior *everywhere* in the school; and (4) the students are expected to transfer their skills across people and settings.

Training is generally needed to ensure that everyone in a building understands and can implement the Stop & Think process. At the very least, paraprofessionals (or teacher assistants), custodians, cafeteria workers, secretaries, and other support personnel should receive a two-hour training session so that (1) they understand the fundamentals of the Stop & Think process and the importance of teaching and reinforcing prosocial behavior; (2) they can comfortably and automatically use the five Stop & Think steps to interact with and guide students when there is an actual or potential problem; and (3) they see themselves as a critical link in the transfer of training process and in the school's goal of developing and implementing a successful student discipline and behavior management program.

More specifically, this training session should:

1. Introduce the Stop & Think process and its use in the classroom

2. Teach participants the five Stop & Think steps and provide opportunities for the participants to practice them so that they can say them in a natural and automatic way

3. Identify typical problem (or near-problem) situations in the areas of the school in which the participants interact with students

4. Provide role-play opportunities of these situations so that the participants become proficient in using the Stop & Think language to respond to typical problems

5. Emphasize that participants should also look for *appropriate* student behavior and should reinforce such behavior using the Stop & Think steps and process

Facilitating Transfer Across Situations

In addition to the suggestions already discussed, you can facilitate the transfer of social skills training by reinforcing the Stop & Think social skills in a number of different classroom contexts. For example, during Reading or Circle Time, you might point out the use, or misuse, of specific social skills by characters in books and discuss the implications of the characters' actions. When discussing certain holidays, you might discuss how different historical or related figures have used (or not used) social skills, such as during President's Week or Thanksgiving. You can explain how the use of social skills can help your students when they are doing a project or activity together. You can have students prepare and act out a play (an activity in which they need to use prosocial skills), discuss their use of social skills in the classroom, draw pictures depicting their use of social skills, prepare bulletin board displays highlighting the use of social skills, or focus on social skills as a part of class outreach projects. Yet another suggestion is to have older students adopt your students as social skills buddies or mentors, on an individual or class-to-class level, and have them reinforce these skills with your students. You might also have parents get involved in Stop & Think community projects as part of a home-school-community effort.

Many suggestions have been made in this section. The following list summarizes these points, as well as provides a few additional points that may help you facilitate your students' transfer of Stop & Think social skills across time, settings, people, and situations:

In the classroom:

- Post Stop & Think signs on each wall of the classroom and on student desks.

- Have students suggest methods of tracking the use of social skills in the classroom and building and implement the best of these suggestions.

- Use social skills as a theme in art projects, when writing experiential reading stories, and so forth.

- When a problem occurs in the classroom or school, use the Stop & Think process to deal with it.

- After your students return to the classroom from P.E., art, music, or other content-related classes, have them report their use (or misuse) of social skills in those settings. Also have them report their use of social skills in the cafeteria and on the bus.

- Begin each day by reminding your students about the social skills that the class is working on and by reviewing the Stop & Think steps.

In the building:

- Set building themes for the year around the use of prosocial skills.

- Place Stop & Think signs in strategic places, such as in the cafeteria, halls, and gym.

- Have all of the staff reinforce the use of the social skills training, particularly any time that a student informs a staff person that he or she has appropriately used a social skill.

- Set up competitions among classrooms for the most frequent use of social skills. Be sure, however, that every class that reaches the target number of skills will receive the reward. Any class that exceeds that criterion (or the class that performs the best) might receive special recognition. Be sure to control for class size so that larger classes do not automatically win.

Evaluating the Stop & Think Implementation Process

Through much of this manual, social skills instruction has been viewed as a preventative approach. That is, it has been assumed that *all students* need to learn social skills and that *all classroom teachers* need to be teaching and reinforcing these skills. If this is done, students will learn the interpersonal, problem-solving, and conflict resolution skills that they need every day, and this knowledge will help them prevent problems from occurring and will increase their prosocial interactions.

However, there are times when problems will arise involving specific students or situations. At such times, a problem-solving process should be used to functionally (1) identify the problem, (2) analyze the problem, (3) intervene with the problem, and (4) evaluate the impact of the intervention and problem-solving process. If the problem-solving process identifies the Stop & Think process and the teaching of specific social skills as strategically and functionally needed components of the intervention, then social skills instruction should be integrated into this problem-solving orientation.

Whether the Stop & Think process is used in a preventative or problem-solving mode, it needs to be evaluated. Specifically, evaluation should cover the areas of training, implementation and the transfer of training, and behavioral outcomes.

Evaluating Stop & Think Training

In each phase of the Stop & Think instructional process—the teaching of the skill, continued practice during application activities, and ongoing reinforcement during infusion opportunities—the targeted social skill must be taught with integrity. To determine whether this is the case, it is important to evaluate the effectiveness of the teaching lesson, the accurate use of the Stop & Think language and specific skill script, the quality of the modeling and role plays used, and the correct use of the performance feedback provided to the students. Detailed evaluation forms for teacher performance in these areas are available from the publishers.

Evaluating Stop & Think Implementation and the Transfer of Training

This manual has emphasized the importance of teachers and other staff prompting, reinforcing, and eliciting Stop & Think skills across time, settings, people, and situations. To evaluate how well the skills are being implemented for real-life situations and the transfer of training process is being facilitated, two approaches can be used: observation and interview or survey feedback. Initially, an effective evaluation involves self-observation and self-recording by teachers. These evaluations then can be qualitatively extended through interviews or surveys.

An example of a self-observation protocol that can help you track your and others' transfer of training implementation across time, settings, people, and situations is included in *Stop & Think Reproducible Forms*. Also available from the publisher is a sample teacher evaluation survey for the same four dimensions.

Evaluating Stop & Think Behavioral Outcomes

The final aspect that must be evaluated is the outcome of the Stop & Think process. That is, how well are your students using different social skills to get along with one another, to problem solve through social and other situations, and to resolve conflicts before they occur, as they are about to occur, and even after they occur? These outcomes can be evaluated by considering a spectrum of related behavioral responses ranging from (1) students' ability to appropriately respond to an external prompt (i.e., from a teacher, another adult, or even a peer) with a prosocial skill to (2) their ability to prompt themselves and use the Stop & Think process with a prosocial skill to (3) their ability to independently and automatically use a prosocial skill in response to a specific situation to (4) their ability to prompt and reinforce prosocial skills in other students. These outcomes can also be evaluated by tracking the number of times a classroom lesson or activity is disrupted by a student's Bad Choice, or by the number of discipline referrals to a building principal. Regardless, as always when considering these outcomes, the developmental, maturational, and situational contexts of the students must be taken into account.

A brief survey that can be used to evaluate Stop & Think behavioral outcomes is included in *Stop & Think Reproducible Forms*. The survey can be supplemented by behavioral observations of specific students who are not demonstrating the expected behavioral outcomes of this program as well as by behavior rating scales that evaluate individual students or groups of students across numerous expected behaviors inside and outside the classroom.

Some General Reminders

Remember, it's hard to be a student in today's world. There are so many pressures and so many inappropriate models. The Stop & Think process, along with a good accountability system of meaningful incentives and consequences and consistency over time, can help you teach your students how to make better choices and become better self-managers. But the Stop & Think process, like anything else, takes time, effort, and persistence.

Students have many important choices and decisions to make, and they will continue to have to make important choices and decisions throughout their lives. The Stop & Think process has helped many students to be more successful in the interpersonal, problem-solving, and conflict resolution areas that directly relate to these choices and decisions.

Remember, the key to the Stop & Think process is to teach your students—step by step—how to perform the behaviors that you expect. Throughout this manual, you have learned that:

- You need to teach each social skill directly using the steps provided.

- You need to use the same script to guide your students through each specific social skill every time you practice.

- You need to correctly demonstrate the social skill that you are teaching using real-life situations that occur at school and then have your students practice the skill until they can perform it with less and less prompting.

- You need to consistently use the Stop & Think steps and the social skills scripts in your classroom, and you need to consistently give your students incentives to make Good Choices and consequences when making Bad Choices.

- Finally, you need to help your students use the skills in different places, with different people, and at different times of the day.

If you follow the *Stop & Think Social Skills Program*, you will help your students to be more successful in the classroom and school and also at home and in the community. You will help them to acquire skills that will benefit them for the rest of their lives.

Appendices

Appendix A:
Overview of Project ACHIEVE

Appendix B:
Essential Readings

Appendix C:
Glossary

Appendix A: Overview of Project ACHIEVE

Project ACHIEVE, developed by Drs. Howard Knoff and George Batsche at the University of South Florida, is an innovative educational reform program targeting academically and socially at-risk and underachieving students. Project ACHIEVE began as a districtwide training program for school psychologists, guidance counselors, social workers, and elementary-level instructional consultants.

Project ACHIEVE is now a school-based/whole-school professional development program that teaches and reinforces critical staff skills and intervention approaches that focus on helping staff to strategically plan for and address the immediate and long-term academic and behavioral needs of students. More specifically, Project ACHIEVE places particular emphasis on increasing student performance in the areas of social skills and conflict resolution, improving student achievement and academic progress, facilitating positive school climates, and increasing parental involvement and support. To effect these changes an integrated process is used that involves organizational and resource development, comprehensive inservice training and follow-up, and parent and community involvement, all leading to direct and preventive services for our at-risk students.

There are seven interdependent components to Project ACHIEVE: (1) strategic planning and organizational analysis and development; (2) a referral question consultation (RQC) process; (3) effective classroom teaching/staff development; (4) instructional consultation and curriculum-based assessment; (5) behavioral consultation and behavioral interventions, including the schoolwide and parent/community use of social skills (or problem solving) and aggression control training; (6) parent training, tutoring, and support; and (7) research and accountability. These components, which are described in detail later in this Appendix, are supported by four interdependent conceptual models that guide all of our practice.

The Conceptual Models Underlying Project ACHIEVE

The four conceptual models that guide the implementation of Project ACHIEVE at its systems, building, academic, and behavioral levels are (1) the Strategic Planning model; (2) the Organizational and Integrated Services model; (3) the Problem-Solving and Student Learning and

Instruction model; and (4) the School Safety and Effective Behavior Management model.

Briefly, the foundation to the **Strategic Planning model** is the recognition that organizational change and strategic planning are natural, necessary, and ongoing processes in any healthy organization and that some seemingly child-focused problems in our schools are actually building, systems, or community problems that must be addressed at multiple levels using a problem-solving process that results in systematic, multifaceted intervention and substantive change. Strategic planning thus often proceeds through the following five phases: creating a base for planning and change; developing a strategic plan; developing an implementation plan; implementing and monitoring the plan; and renewing the plan. More specifically, this process involves the identification of student, staff, parent, and community needs; environmental and organizational analyses that identify differential strengths, weaknesses, resources, and limitations; the identification of organizational visions and mission, along with long-term and short-term goals and desired outcomes; and the development of annual action plans that specify objectives, activities, implementation timelines, needed resources, and evaluation approaches. All of this is done by coordinating the change process with a district's various planning and budgeting cycles and by analyzing the dynamics of the district through review of its receiving system, performance system, human resources and people system, and pervasive system variables.

The foundation to the **Organizational and Integrated Services model** is five components that can facilitate the integration and planning of a systematic **and systemic** change process for public school districts. Critical here is the notion that any effective systems change process, like Project ACHIEVE, needs "top-down" administrative approval and support in order to effect the "bottom-up" functional implementation at the building level. In addition, the importance of an integrated system across regular, compensatory, and special education—including pupil personnel services and safe and drug-free schools—must be noted. The five components of this model are finance and funding, administration and policy, professional training and competency, service delivery, and research, evaluation, and program evaluation. These five components involve a number of principles and procedures that help to operationalize the strategic planning process described above.

The foundation to the **Problem-Solving and Student Learning and Instruction model** is the referral question consultation process. The RQC process is an empirically based, generic problem-solving model that can be used for specific academic and behavioral problems. More refined than the traditional generic problem-solving models that encourage problem identification, problem analysis, intervention, and evaluation steps, the RQC is an assessment approach that is directly and functionally linked to intervention. Described simply, the RQC process employs the scientific method in an empirically based, hypothesis-generating and testing search for *why* a referred problem is occurring. The five primary areas considered in the RQC process to help explain why students have academic or behavioral difficulties are student characteristics and/or conditions; teacher and/or instructional environment characteristics or conditions; curricular characteristics or conditions; classroom, school building, district characteristics or conditions; and family, neighborhood, and/or community characteristics or conditions.

Relative to student learning, the problem-solving process looks at the student, the teacher and instructional process, and the curriculum. That is, if a student is *not* achieving satisfactorily, the problem-solving assessment looks at the contribution of the student, the teaching, and the curriculum to the "problem" at hand. Beyond these three components, environmental factors within the classroom and the school, as well as home or community factors, may also be impacting the learning process. These latter factors, however, impact student achievement only indirectly. Many students are able to overcome the impact of adverse home, school, and classroom environments because they have sound self-management, motivation, and/or self-competency skills, or because of a strong teacher and/or curriculum.

The foundation to the **School Safety and Effective Behavior Management model** is a systems approach that focuses on the organizational requirements and processes that result in effective buildingwide prosocial behavior management and positive, skills-oriented student discipline systems. The three primary components needed for any successful school discipline and behavior management system are (1) the development of student and staff skills that result in students' demonstrating prosocial interpersonal, problem-solving, and conflict resolution skills; (2) the development of teacher, grade-level, and buildingwide accountability systems; and (3) the development of staff and administrative consistency patterns such that student behavior is reinforced and consequenced in a constant fashion.

Beyond this, the model extends to analyses of "special situations" — buildingwide behavioral situations involving problems that occur in a school's more public areas and that involve students but are not completely caused by or solved through interventions focusing only on these students. Often, these special situations involve problems in such places as the school's cafeteria, hallways, buses, recess or playgrounds, media centers, and other "common" areas. These special situations are analyzed by considering the following domains: (1) student characteristics, issues, and factors; (2) teacher/staff characteristics, issues, and factors; (3) environmental characteristics, issues, and factors (physical plant and logistics); (4) incentives and consequences; and (5) resources.

Finally, this model emphasizes the need for school districts and buildings to have prevention, intervention, and crisis response teams that focus on overall school safety. These district- and building-level teams should include administrators, staff, students, parents, and relevant community leaders; and they should develop plans and procedures to prevent and respond to potential crisis situations. These situations might include racial, multicultural, and diversity issues; school violence and weapons issues; drug and alcohol issues; tolerance and harassment issues; mental health, depression, and suicide issues; and life transitions and family crisis issues.

Project ACHIEVE Goals, Components, and Implementation Blueprint

Project ACHIEVE has been implemented in all types of schools across the country, most often in schools with a high number of at-risk children and youth. These include schoolwide Chapter 1 schools, schools participating in full-service school programs, schools with large numbers of special education referrals each year, and schools at risk for multiple incidents of violence. At the present time, many of the schools participating in this project are Title I schoolwide or full-service schools. There are, however, other schools and districts that participate in Project ACHIEVE training because they want to prevent future problems or because they want to build on the strengths of their already-existing program.

Regardless of the setting, Project ACHIEVE has six primary goals:

1. To enhance the problem-solving skills of teachers so that effective interventions for social difficulties (in particular, violence) and academic difficulties of at-risk students are developed and implemented.

2. To improve the building and classroom management skills of school personnel and the behavior of students (i.e., to reduce antisocial and increase prosocial behaviors) through the use of a building-based social skills and aggression control training program in order to create a disciplined environment within which students can learn (increased academic engaged time).

3. To improve the school's comprehensive services to students with below-average academic performance so that they are served, as much as possible, in the regular classroom setting and have equal access to high quality educational programs. This goal is based on the assumption that students who can succeed in an environment are less likely to act out against that environment. Violence prevention/intervention programs must address the academic component of educational settings.

4. To increase the social and academic progress of students through enhanced involvement of parents and the community in the education of their children, specifically through their direct involvement with the schoolwork of their children and youth. Fundamental to this increased involvement is the development of improved parenting skills and community-based academic support activities.

5. To validate the various components of Project ACHIEVE and to develop demonstration training sites for district personnel with the purpose of expanding this model to other school settings.

6. To create a school climate in which each teacher, staff member, and parent believes that everyone is responsible for every student in that building and community.

The Project ACHIEVE Components

As noted earlier, seven interdependent components make up Project ACHIEVE: (1) strategic planning and organizational analysis and development; (2) a referral question consultation (RQC) process; (3) effective classroom teaching/staff development; (4) instructional consultation and curriculum-based assessment; (5) behavioral consultation and behavioral interventions, including the schoolwide and parent/community use of social skills (or problem solving) and aggression control training; (6) parent training, tutoring, and support; and (7) research and accountability. These components are described immediately below.

1. The **strategic planning and organizational analysis and development component** initially focuses on assessing the organizational climate, administrative style, staff decision-making, and other interactive processes at a Project ACHIEVE school and moves eventually and as needed into the development of new organizational patterns and interactions that facilitate and support the academic and social progress of the school's student body. The analysis and strategic planning are accomplished through

community, environmental, and organizational needs assessment procedures and techniques; evaluations of the current efficacy of existing student assessment and intervention programs; and the initiation of strategic planning processes through one-, three-, and five-year action plans. In developing these action plans, Project ACHIEVE helps schools to target and assess their own strengths, weaknesses, threats, and opportunities and to build educational reform processes that are strategically tailored to their individual goals and capabilities. Significantly, systematic organizational assessment and strategic planning are the foundations to the entire school reform/planned change process relative to student achievement and success.

In summary, the strategic planning and organizational analysis and development component uses systematic strategic planning to assess targeted facets of the organization; to identify organizational strengths, weaknesses, opportunities, and threats; to generate specific programmatic objectives and action plans; and to coordinate evaluation procedures that measure goal progress and attainment.

2. The **referral question consultation process component** is grounded in the belief that school systems and building staff must utilize a common language and method of problem solving in order to address potential or referred problems. Thus, Project ACHIEVE trains all of the professional and support staff in a building to use the referral question consultation (RQC) process. The RQC problem-solving approach uses the scientific method in an empirically based search for why a referred student-specific problem is occurring. After behaviorally clarifying the presenting problem, the RQC process focuses on functionally explaining and confirming why the referred problem is occurring, so that effective interventions to resolve the student's problem and to facilitate continued academic and social progress ultimately can be developed. Overall, the RQC method requires school professionals to complete functional analyses of referral problems in the environments where they occur. The RQC training facilitates a conceptual shift in the service-delivery philosophy of the building from a refer-test-place approach to one of problem-solving, consultation, and classroom-based intervention.

In summary, the referral question consultation process component uses a systematic, problem-solving process that provides the foundation for every consultation interaction, whether child-focused, teacher- or parent-focused, or program- or system-focused. This process focuses on explaining why student problems are occurring and on functionally linking assessment to intervention, resulting in real student progress.

3. The **effective classroom teacher/staff development component** focuses on training staff to ensure that effective instructional styles and teaching behaviors, as well as appropriate curricular procedures and materials, are used in the classroom. The goal is to maximize students' attention to task, academic engaged time, academic learning time, and, ultimately, their specific and general achievement. This is accomplished by providing teachers with appropriate inservice instruction, opportunities for practice, and clinical supervision so that the many effective teaching techniques that maximize students' educational and social progress are mastered and continuously used. In all, 12 effective instruction clusters are used in this Project ACHIEVE component. Specifically, they focus on instructional match, teacher expectations, classroom environment, instructional presentation, cognitive emphasis, motivational strategies, relevant practice, informed feedback, academic engaged time, adaptive instruction, progress evaluation, and student understanding. After training, supervision is done using a clinical supervision model such that professional development teams are created in each school to provide feedback and skill-building opportunities for all teachers and other staff.

   In summary, the effective classroom teacher/staff development component focuses on developing and reinforcing those classroom-based teacher/instructional behaviors that maximize students' time on task, academic engagement, and academic learning time. This component includes the development and supervision of those behaviors that help to effectively match students with specific and effective curricula.

4. The **instructional consultation and curriculum-based assessment to intervention component** focuses on the belief that the learner is part of an instructional system that involves interdependent interactions between task demands (i.e., What needs to be learned?), the instruction (i.e., Are appropriate instructional and management strategies available and being used?), and the student (i.e., Is the student ready and capable of learning?). Critically, the link between assessment and intervention is paramount. The assessment of students' learning status and progress is accomplished by evaluating (1) the match between the students and the processes used by the curriculum to facilitate learning, the students' ability to succeed in the curriculum, and their progress in the curriculum; (2) the quality of instruction and the presence/absence of effective school and schooling

characteristics as they relate to student learning and achievement; and (3) the curriculum itself—its development, technical adequacy, task demands, encouragement of sound instruction, and impact on learning.

In this context, Project ACHIEVE has adopted a functional, curriculum-based assessment and intervention approach to student achievement that uses, as much as possible, direct instruction and a mastery-model perspective of academic outcomes. Teachers are taught how to identify and analyze curricular and instructional variables and their relationship to student achievement outcomes, how to assess curricular (i.e., scope and sequence) placement and performance expectations, and how to complete curricular task analyses so that assessment is functionally linked to intervention in the classroom. Additionally, research results from learning theory and practice are integrated into the classroom to enhance the learning environment and process and to facilitate more positive outcomes.

Another critical part of this component focuses on the development and implementation of a curriculum-based measurement (CBM) system that includes the generation of local norms of achievement in the areas of reading, mathematics, spelling, and written expression and/or the use of CBM materials to evaluate intervention efficacy and to monitor individual student progress. With these CBM norms, a teacher can assess specific students and compare them to same-aged peers to help identify those who are at risk and underachieving. Using the CBM probes, teachers can collect multiple samples of individual students' work that they can more functionally assess and track these students' academic progress over time. When integrated into the broader curriculum-based assessment and RQC processes, all of this results in (1) more functional assessments that identify why a student is having academic difficulties, (2) curricular interventions and curricular consultation directions that are linked to the assessment process and have a higher probability of success, and, as a result, (3) more successful instructional programs for at-risk and underachieving students.

In summary, the instructional consultation and curriculum-based assessment to intervention component focuses on the functional, curriculum-based assessment of referred students' learning problems by evaluating students' progress in and response to the curriculum, their ability to succeed in the curriculum, and the instructional processes needed for them to achieve skill mastery.

5. The **social skills, behavioral consultation, and behavioral interventions component** focuses on the analysis and implementation of effective behavioral interventions that are designed to resolve students' curricular and behavioral problems or to improve teachers' instructional and classroom management procedures. These interventions, therefore, focus on specific referred problems exhibited by students in the school or classroom (e.g., not completing homework, noncompliance, swearing, threatening others) or specific behaviors that, inappropriately, are or are not exhibited by teachers as part of the instructional process (e.g., not providing advanced organizers or appropriate instructional feedback, reinforcing inappropriate behavior through attention, using discipline inconsistently). Teachers are taught to strategically choose from among the following behavioral approaches within the context of the student's behavioral ecology: direct instruction of the skill, stimulus control approaches, behavioral addition approaches, behavioral reduction approaches, behavioral maintenance approaches, and behavioral generalization approaches. At the same time, support staff are taught specific behavioral observation, data collection, consultation intervention, and intervention evaluation strategies and techniques.

A critical part of this behavioral consultation/intervention component involves the instruction of prosocial skills using social learning theory principles and our Stop & Think social skills training approach. Project ACHIEVE's Stop & Think social skills training provides students with over 60 behavioral skills (e.g., listening, following directions, asking and responding to questions and requests) that facilitate positive student behavior and motivation and thus increase time on task and academic engagement. Focusing on survival, interpersonal, problem-solving, academic support, and conflict resolution skills, this training prevents or resolves many student behavior problems, and it helps to change the entire school climate in a way that the school becomes a more positive and safer place.

In summary, the social skills, behavioral consultation, and behavioral interventions component focuses on the implementation of effective behavioral interventions to address students' curricular and behavioral problems and/or teachers' instructional and classroom management procedures. The cornerstone of this component is the schoolwide and parent use of social skills training; the development of classroom, grade-level, and buildingwide accountability systems; and the use of "special situation" analyses and school prevention, intervention, and crisis response teams. The social skills and intervention training provides students with specific procedures and behavioral skills to help them to confront and resolve social situations that involve conflict, interpersonal challenges, academic expectations, and other behavioral problems. This training is typically done by teachers who teach and reinforce the skills in the classroom as well as by parents at home. In addition, this training is schoolwide to the extent that all staff (including bus drivers, cafeteria workers, and custodians) are trained in and reinforce the social skills steps and procedures.

6. The **parent training, tutoring, and support component** focuses on increasing the involvement of all parents in all facets of Project ACHIEVE, with a special focus on increasing the involvement of the parents of at-risk, underachieving, and special education students. Parental involvement in the school and educational process often occurs less in the homes of these students, and it is a variable that directly differentiates achieving (or progressing) from underachieving students. This component of Project ACHIEVE involves (1) direct training of target students' parents in tutoring strategies, in parts of their child's classroom curriculum, and in positive behavior management approaches; (2) direct supervision of the parents-in-training through a "Parents in the Classroom" program, where the parents work with students who have academic difficulties like their own child's; (3) direct supervision of the parents-in-training through a "Parents and Their Children" program, in which the parents work with their own child in the educational setting; (4) direct consultation with the parents-in-training in their home settings following program training; and (5) the creation of Parent Drop-In Centers to encourage parent participation in school activities and parent access to training and learning materials.

    In summary, the parent training, tutoring, and support component focuses on the development of ongoing home-school collaboration by (1) making parents an integral part of the planning and activities of the school, (2) helping parents to understand teachers' expectations of their children and to increase their support of their children's academic and social development, (3) increasing parent-to-parent communication and resource building, and (4) supporting parent-to-teacher collaboration so as to build effective home-school partnerships.

7. The **research and accountability component** focuses on the project's active research program investigating critical consultation and/or curricular and behavioral intervention variables and techniques. Part of this research involves collecting specific

formative and summative outcome data on various aspects of Project ACHIEVE, including the RQC process, the inservice training components, the training and implementation of curriculum/behavioral interventions, and the effectiveness of school reform activities for referred students and their teachers and/or systems. Another part of this research involves an ongoing investigation of consultation effectiveness and the organizational, classroom, and interpersonal characteristics that predict and influence consultation success. Overall, this component provides ongoing feedback on the time- and cost-effectiveness of Project ACHIEVE. It also provides formative evaluation feedback such that the project can be adapted at the building level with greater effectiveness and accountability.

In summary, the research and accountability component involves collecting specific data on all aspects of PROJECT ACHIEVE's components and program.

How the Stop & Think Teachers' Manuals Fit Into the Project ACHIEVE Blueprint

The Stop & Think teachers' manuals consist of four separate but related manuals that are written for teachers who have students at the preschool through early elementary, early elementary through middle elementary, middle elementary through late elementary, and middle school/early adolescent age (or developmental) levels. These Stop & Think teachers' manuals fit into the *Social Skills, Behavioral Consultation, and Behavioral Interventions and Effective School Instructional Practices and Staff Development* components of Project ACHIEVE. More specifically, these Stop & Think teachers' manuals help teachers to teach their students the important interpersonal, problem-solving, and conflict resolution skills that will help them to be socially successful at school. As these skills are reinforced at school and at home, they will also help students to become effective self-managers in the classroom and to demonstrate the academic engagement and motivation that result in sound learning and positive academic outcomes.

The Stop & Think teachers' manuals are also a critical element in achieving the ultimate goals of Project ACHIEVE's *Social Skills, Discipline/Behavior Management, and School Safety System* over a two-year period of implementation. These goals are:

1. To prepare every teacher in a school building to effectively teach social skills to his or her students on a bimonthly basis in his or her classroom;

2. To prepare every other staff person in the building with the skills and resources to support and reinforce this classroom-based instruction;

3. To develop and implement a classroom-level, grade-level, and buildingwide accountability system that extends the social skills process to include an educative time-out process while identifying expected student behavior (with corresponding incentives) and different levels of inappropriate student behavior (with corresponding consequences);

4. To create a staff support and reinforcement infrastructure that helps staff to feel comfortable and competent with the social skills and time-out processes and that encourages the consistent use of the social skills and accountability systems developed;

5. To establish a data management system that can track the outcomes and success of the program at student, teacher, grade, and building levels;

6. To form a School Climate or Disciplinary Committee that can analyze building-level "special situations," develop and implement crisis prevention and response plans and approaches, and coordinate additional behavioral intervention training and resources for classroom teachers; and

7. To involve students, parents, community agencies and programs, and other community leaders in a collaborative effort that supports all of the goals above and that extends Project ACHIEVE's training and implementation to home and community.

In the end, if these goals are accomplished, then the following outcomes should occur:

1. Significant reductions in student discipline problems referred to the office.

2. Significant reductions in the number of student suspensions and expulsions.

3. Increased levels of positive reinforcement for students who are demonstrating appropriate behavior and making prosocial choices.

4. Increased levels of student academic engagement.

5. Increased levels of consistency across teachers and staff in classrooms and throughout the building in dealing with student behavior and behavior problems.

6. A more positive and supportive school climate across students and staff.

7. More parents and community programs using the social skills process and linking the school's discipline, behavior management, and safety approaches with their own.

Appendix B: Essential Readings

Understanding the Impact of Child Development on the Social Skills Teaching Process

During the preschool through early elementary years, children develop in a number of very significant ways. Some of the developmental changes that these children experience include:

1. Continued slow growth in height, weight, and body proportion.

2. Ongoing brain development that helps them to increase their language skills and to acquire more advanced fine and gross motor skills.

3. Increased ability to learn from and respond to different environments. This begins with children focusing on themselves and moves to include their ability to understand others' perspectives.

4. Social development such that they become increasingly independent—wanting to do more things for themselves, to explore and control their own surroundings, and to interact with others in play and group situations.

Despite all of this growth, you need to have realistic expectations of what your students can learn and how quickly. In general, all students have the capacity to learn the Stop & Think process, but how quickly they learn these skills and how well they use them in real life will vary considerably.

When teaching social skills to students at the preschool to early elementary school ages, you need to make sure that your instruction is specific, step by step, repetitive, and predictable and that it uses role-plays or practice examples that ensure a high level of success. As long as you see your preschool to early elementary school students responding to the Stop & Think steps more quickly and in a wider range of settings and situations, you should consider your social skills instruction successful.

Preschool to early elementary school students will rarely initiate their own practice of new social skills, but they will increasingly use the Stop & Think language and the social skills behavior for skills that teachers continuously practice with them and reinforce. Further, preschool to early elementary school students will rarely prompt, begin, monitor, evaluate, or reinforce their own social skills behavior. Self-management skills need to be taught to these students. Because these self-management skills often are not fully mastered until early adolescence, teachers must continue to provide the prompts and guidance these young students will need to practice, develop, and master the social skills they teach.

As a teacher of preschool to early elementary school students, you can use four sequential steps, over time, to help your students increase their ability to use the social skills scripts and behaviors more independently. These four steps are:

- Step 1: Verbalize the Stop & Think process and prompt your students to repeat the steps out loud.

- Step 2: Verbalize the Stop & Think process and prompt your students to repeat the steps in a whisper voice (subvocalizing).

- Step 3: Cue the Stop & Think process (with a physical, visual, or verbal cue) and prompt your students to repeat the steps out loud.

- Step 4: Cue the Stop & Think process (with a physical, visual, or verbal cue) and prompt your students to repeat the steps in a whisper voice (subvocalizing).

Realistically, preschoolers and kindergarten students will probably be able to respond only to Steps 1 and 2, while early elementary students should be able to respond to all four steps over time.

Teachers of middle and late elementary school students would continue to use these steps but would also encourage the use of the following steps as soon as possible:

- Step 5: Students prompt themselves and verbalize the Stop & Think process out loud.

- Step 6: Students prompt themselves and verbalize the Stop & Think process in a whisper voice (subvocalizing).

- Step 7: Students prompt themselves and verbalize the Stop & Think process inside their heads.

- Step 8: Students perform the Stop & Think process at an automatic or mastery level.

It is important to note that students are not able to prompt themselves until they become aware of how situations are affecting them *before* they behaviorally react. This awareness involves **Situational Awareness** and **Physical or Self-Awareness**. **Situational Awareness** occurs when students can identify the people, places, times, activities, and other situations (the **triggers**) that cause the most difficulty for them. **Physical**

or Self-Awareness occurs when students can identify their physical and emotional reactions, or **cues**, to these difficult situations (e.g., what they say inside their heads, how they emotionally feel, the ways that their bodies react internally) *before* they behaviorally respond. These reactions cue students that they are responding to a situation and may need to use the Stop & Think process to make a Good Choice.

Remember that preschool through early elementary students do not independently prompt themselves. Although they have triggers and cues, they are not consciously aware of them. As a teacher, you can use the Stop & Think process and language, over time, to teach these students about their triggers and cues by verbally identifying them as they occur. As students grow older, they begin to understand and associate these triggers and cues with different Good Choice and Bad Choice situations. Eventually, with experiences and maturation, they become independently aware of their own triggers and cues and how to use them within the Stop & Think process.

Without the Stop & Think training, any of a number of situations that commonly occur in the classroom or within the school can trigger students' emotional and/or Bad Choice responses. The following "Trigger Box" lists some of the typical triggers of Bad Choice behavior at the preschool through early elementary school level. If any other triggers are specific or different for your students, feel free to add to or modify this list.

The Trigger Box

Following is a list of situations that often trigger emotional responses in preschool through early elementary school students:

- Being teased
- Losing a game
- Getting a bad grade
- Not getting the teacher's attention
- Not getting their way
- Being frustrated with schoolwork
- Being rejected or left out
- Feeling unjustly accused or blamed
- Feeling that the teacher is being unfair
- Having to share
- Having to clean up or stop an activity
- Hearing a specific word or phrase
- Hearing a specific tone of voice, intonation, or inflection

Some of the typical cues (i.e., physical or emotional reactions) that students at this age level experience when they are in difficult situations are listed in the following "Cue Box." If any other cues are specific or different for your students, feel free to add to or modify this list.

The Cue Box

Here is a list of physical or self-awareness cues that preschool through early elementary school students often experience when in emotional situations:

- Sweating or getting hot
- Making a repetitive movement (e.g., clenching fists over and over again)
- Being unable to think
- Being unable to see clearly
- Having heart or pulse race
- Feeling sick
- Feeling tingly all over
- Wanting to run away
- Wanting to scream or hit someone
- Remembering a past emotional situation
- Hearing a phrase or sound inside their heads over and over again
- Repeating a negative statement in their heads over and over again

---

Critically, you need to help your students learn to **Stop and Think** before they get too emotional or out of control when they are involved in a difficult situation. One way to do this, as shown in the following script, is to verbally identify students' triggers and cues, thus helping to teach students that these triggers and cues exist and are influencing their behavior:

> David, I can see that you are starting to get upset about being behind everyone on this assignment (**trigger**). I can hear your voice getting louder and angrier, and you are starting to look more upset and to make more mistakes and erasures (**cues**). David, you need to **Stop and Think** and take a deep breath so you can calm down. **Are you going to make a Good Choice or a Bad Choice?** If you make a Good Choice and calm down, you can get the assignment done more quickly and with more correct responses. After all, the most important thing is to learn the material correctly so that we can build on it later. It's okay that you're a little behind. That happens to everyone at some point. But, if you make a Bad Choice and get too upset, I'll have to stop you from completing this work and then you'll be even more behind. I think you want to make a Good Choice so that you can finish your assignment, but let's see. David, do you want to make a Good Choice or a Bad Choice?

When students are aware of both their triggers and their cues, they can use the Stop & Think process to (1) keep themselves in emotional control, (2) stop an inappropriate response to a difficult situation, and (3) go through the steps toward making a Good Choice. This, however, is a learning process, and you are instrumental in this process. Over time, as students move through the eight steps listed previously, their behavior will become conditioned to these triggers and cues such that they will behaviorally respond with Good Choices more automatically.

The presence of so many emotional situations in students' lives is one reason why the first Stop & Think step (**Stop and Think!**) is emphasized so much. When students are in a stressful situation that requires a particular interpersonal, problem-solving, or conflict resolution response, the **Stop and Think** step helps them to stay in control of the situation. This helps them to then make a Good Choice when it might be easier to react more immediately or impulsively with an ineffective Bad Choice.

All students need a great deal of teacher instruction, support, and guidance before they will begin to use the Stop & Think process more independently, automatically, and routinely. As you move from teaching the various social skills to day-to-day use and practice of them within the Stop & Think process, you will be more successful if you do the following:

- Verbally (and sometimes physically) guide your students through the social skills steps.

- Use hand signals to prompt the five Stop & Think steps along with the social skills language.

- Be realistic as to how quickly and automatically your students will learn these social skills but have high and reasonable expectations for their progress.

- Positively reinforce your students and reward them for improvements in learning and using the Stop & think process over time.

- Show your students your confidence in their success.

- Transfer your students' training by providing them opportunities to practice and master skills at different times of the day, in different settings, with different people, in different situations, and under different conditions.

Accountability: Giving Students Incentives and Consequences

Accountability has been discussed in a number of different places in this manual. Because creating and maintaining a meaningful accountability system is so important to teaching success, this reading begins with a review of the important points about accountability that have been discussed thus far.

Important Considerations in Creating a Meaningful Accountability System

- You need to provide your students with **meaningful** incentives and consequences to motivate them toward Good Choices and away from Bad Choices, respectively. When your students have mastered their social skills and they know that you will consistently apply incentives and consequences, they generally will make Good Choices because they know they will be positively reinforced after making those choices.

- Incentives and consequences must be developmentally appropriate for the age and maturation level of the student, and they should be used only to the degree needed for success.

- All students, regardless of their age, gender, or special circumstances, need to be in environments that provide five positive interactions for every negative interaction (see 5-to-1 Rule described later in this Appendix). This also means that every consequence experienced by a student should be offset by five positive reinforcements. Both research and practice have shown that students learn and develop most favorably in environments that provide five positive interactions for every negative interaction.

- Meaningful incentives typically are identified by (1) observing what objects, activities, or interactions your students enjoy most; (2) asking other teachers with same-aged students what the peer group is currently "into"; and/or (3) watching TV to see what games or products are currently popular.

- The best incentives are personal, intrinsic, and interactive: a pat on the back or special compliment, time spent together, art and other supplies to be used for creative projects, or a book or computer opportunities that can be educational and fun.

- When you use tangible or overt incentives, pair these extrinsic reinforcers with social reinforcers (such as giving your student a pat on the back) and intrinsic reinforcers (such as positive self-statements like: "Tell yourself you did a Great Job!" or "Give yourself a big pat on the back for making such a Good Choice!"). Over time, this will help students to become more responsive to social and intrinsic reinforcers and less dependent on tangible reinforcers that sometimes get out of control as students expect more and more "perks." Ultimately, the goal is for students to be predominantly intrinsically and self-motivated.

- Consequences are not the same as punishment. Punishment is meant to stop inappropriate behavior from happening again. Consequences are meant to motivate Good Choices and appropriate behavior and to discourage Bad Choices as the student focuses on avoiding additional consequences.

- Like incentives, meaningful consequences are identified by observing what objects, activities, or interactions your students enjoy most and by asking other teachers with same-aged students what their students enjoy. Typical consequences at this age level include correcting, fixing, or restoring an offense or damage; needing to positively practice the appropriate behavior (that did not originally occur) numerous times; loss of positive teacher attention; loss of an opportunity to participate in an activity or an incentive opportunity; loss of privileges; or a time-out.

- As much as possible, use logical or natural consequences. Logical consequences are logically tied or related to the specific situation where the student made a Bad Choice. If a student did not use the

Waiting for Your Turn skill appropriately, examples of some logical consequences might be: (1) telling the student you cannot talk or respond to him or her for a specific period of time, even after the waiting time is over; (2) having the student practice the **Waiting for Your Turn** skill an extra three to five minutes after the situation is over; or (3) having the student lose a turn if the situation involves a game or activity.

Natural consequences occur almost automatically as a result of a student's inappropriate behavior. Examples include (1) a student having to redo a worksheet because he or she did not follow directions appropriately, (2) a student missing a favorite classroom activity because he or she did not listen to know where and when the activity would occur, (3) peers refusing to play with another student because he or she did not share materials in the past.

- When using consequences, the mildest possible consequence that will motivate a student's Good Choice should be used. For some students, consequences need to be at the same level of intensity as, or more intense than, previous consequences for the consequences to be meaningful. Unfortunately, this often results in a "death spiral," where teachers are continually increasing the intensity of their consequences in order to maintain a basic level of behavioral control.

- After you have taught the **Accepting Consequences** skill, your students should use this skill whenever you need to deliver a consequence to them.

- When delivering a consequence, you need to use the Stop & Think script and remember to use a firm yet matter-of-fact voice with your students. Consequences should not be given in an excessively angry or loud voice because the student then might react to the emotion in your voice, forgetting that he or she has made a Bad Choice. If an angry voice is used, the student may refuse to follow or accept the consequence, avoid responsibility for the Bad Choice, and then blame you for yelling or getting angry with him or her.

- Praise your students after they have accepted and followed your consequences. Even though you may still be disappointed that a student made a Bad Choice, it is important to recognize that he or she is taking responsibility for his or her behavior and is trying to make things better. Praise at this point will reestablish the more positive tone that you want as you try to move the situation toward a final resolution.

- After students have finished their consequences, they need to practice the Good Choice that they should have made originally. This principle can be summarized by the phrase: "If you consequate, you must educate" (see further discussion later in this Appendix). Thus, two to three Good Choice or positive practice opportunities should occur as soon as possible after the consequences are over and things have calmed down. These positive practices will help increase the probability that Good Choices will be made the next time.

- Make sure your students have learned, practiced, and mastered the social skills you have chosen *before* you use incentives or consequences to motivate their use. Once skills are mastered, students are best motivated to use these skills when they are positively reinforced five times for every one negative consequence.

- If incentives and consequences are applied *before* skills are mastered, students cannot successfully demonstrate those skills and will react with frustration, anger, withdrawal, resistance, and eventually noncompliance or nonresponsiveness. This is called "learned helplessness," and it is very difficult to reverse. However, if incentives and consequences are used *after* social skills are well taught and mastered, then students will use them effectively, making primarily Good Choice or prosocial decisions.

- In addition, you need to understand that consequences may not work immediately. If a student comes from a very inconsistent environment or developmental history, he or she may not believe that you will actually follow through with a stated consequence. Even when you do follow through the first or second time, the student may still be expecting (based on past history) that you will not follow through the next time. Over time, however, as you consistently follow through with appropriate consequences as needed, students will realize that Bad Choices always result in consequences and that Good Choices are more fun. At this point, your consequences have become meaningful, your behavior has become predictable, and your students will begin to respond more routinely with more prosocial behavior and more independent Good Choices.

The 5-to-1 Rule and Its Implications

Perhaps the most important point related to accountability is that all students, regardless of their age, gender, or special circumstances, need to live and learn in environments that provide *five positive interactions for every negative interaction*. Because there are at least three sources of positive or negative interactions for a student in any school setting—adults, other students or peers, and the students themselves—it is vitally important that you (1) provide as many positive interactions with your students as you can, (2) teach all of the students in your classroom and around your school to be positive to one another and reinforce that behavior, and (3) teach your students to self-reinforce and become positive advocates for themselves.

To better understand the impact of the 5-to-1 Rule, imagine being in a setting where you receive one positive interaction for every negative interaction. Then imagine being approached by someone where you don't know if you are going to have a positive or negative interaction with him or her. What do you assume? Don't you assume, even though you know that half of the time this person will be positive and half of the time negative, that you will have a negative interaction? How do you prepare yourself? Don't you either prepare to back away or defend yourself?

Students are the same way. If they are in schools where they routinely receive half positive and half negative interactions, they learn to expect the negative, and then they either begin to withdraw from many of the social interactions in their lives or become inappropriately aggressive in an attempt to (sometimes prematurely) defend themselves. In a 5-to-1 Rule school environment, students are more positive, they expect to succeed, they know that they will be reinforced for their Good Choices or accomplishments, and/or they are more comfortable and likely to reinforce themselves. Further, in 5-to-1 Rule school environments, the negative feedback students receive becomes more meaningful because it is so rare, and when it occurs students are more motivated to make Good Choices in the future so that they will next earn a positive response.

Some teachers have brought up two interesting concerns when introduced to the 5-to-1 Rule. First, they feel that they should not need to positively reinforce their students. They say, "We expect them to behave appropriately and make Good Choices. We should not have to provide them with any special attention; they should simply do what we say." While this may be true after a student has learned and mastered expected behavior and is internally motivated to demonstrate it over time, it is not true at the beginning of the learning process nor is it true as a basic behavioral principle. Don't we all appreciate positive attention and feedback for a job well done or a kind gesture or act—even after we have mastered that job? Don't we all appreciate—*and aren't we all further motivated by*—positive reinforcement for teaching an effective lesson, for doing a good job during a meeting or when on a committee, or for supporting our colleagues and friends?

Students routinely need this positive attention and feedback, too. Positive attention is part of the teaching process, and you—as the most important person in your students' school lives—must provide positive feedback and attention to ensure good learning. From a behavioral perspective, this positive feedback is sometimes the only way that a student truly knows that he or she is really making a Good Choice and behaving appropriately. Sometimes students make Good Choices but are not sure they are really making Good Choices until they receive their teacher's feedback.

In addition, you need to understand that the absence or lack of negative feedback does not constitute positive feedback for students. Indeed, you need to explicitly, verbally, and physically provide your students with positive feedback, being as specific as possible as to why you are positively reinforcing them. Although you are not solely responsible for providing this feedback or creating positive school and learning environments, if you do not begin and reinforce this process, your students will not do it for one another, and your students will not do it for themselves. As in other teaching situations, your students will imitate what you teach, model, and reinforce over time. If you teach your students what to do but do not model and reinforce the expected behavior, your students will not completely learn it and likely will not perform it.

The second teacher concern relates to punishment. Some teachers believe that the only way to hold students accountable for their Bad Choices is to punish them. It is important to remember that if a student does not have the ability to do something, no amount of punishment will motivate or teach that student to perform the desired task or behavior. Further, oftentimes punishment creates such a negative emotional environment for students that it prevents them from learning or making Good Choices (e.g., due to anger, anxiety, fear, or frustration). That is, sometimes punishment makes students so emotional that they *refuse* to make a Good Choice in the future. At other times, punishment may make a student so anxious about making a Good Choice that the student is *unable* to behave effectively.

If You Consequate, You Must Educate

When students make Bad Choices, adults often respond with consequences. As noted earlier, consequences will be effective and motivate students to make better choices if they are meaningful to the students and delivered in an appropriate fashion. Indeed, meaningful consequences are part of an effective accountability and discipline/behavior management system.

It is vital to remember, however, that "if you consequate, you must educate." That is, if you need to deliver a consequence to a student, you need to follow the consequence, as soon as reasonably possible, with three positive practice educational opportunities. In most cases, these positive practice opportunities center around the behaviors that, if the student had demonstrated them originally, would have constituted a Good Choice and not required a consequence.

For example, if a student made a Bad Choice by not following your direction, you should, as soon as possible after the consequence, have the student practice following the direction (and verbalizing the **Following Directions** skill and script) at least three times. If a student made a Bad Choice by pushing a peer away after being teased, you should, after the consequence, have the student practice the **Dealing With Teasing** skill and script at least three times—perhaps with the student who did the original teasing. Finally, if a student made a Bad Choice by interrupting you inappropriately while you were talking in the hallway to another adult, after the consequence you should have the student practice the **How to Interrupt** skill and script at least three times.

The primary reason to integrate "if you consequate, you must educate" into your teaching relates to the way the brain works. When students demonstrate specific Bad Choices, it is assumed that the learning pathways that "allowed" the behavior are already conditioned in their brains. To increase the probability that a Good Choice will occur the next time, you have to either recondition your student's brain with a new Good Choice pathway or put already existing Good Choice and Bad Choice pathways in competition such that the Good Choice pathway is used the next time. To accomplish this, the student needs to practice the Good Choice behavior (with both the social skill and script) at least three times whenever he or she makes a Bad Choice. This way, the Good Choice behavior is reconditioned or reinforced and is more probable the next time.

In essence, it is important to condition or recondition the neurological pathways that guide your students' behavior. The ultimate goal is to teach your students to demonstrate prosocial behavior such that it is mastered and automatic, to motivate your students to use these behaviors, and to reinforce these behaviors consistently so that your students begin to demonstrate and use these behaviors independently and across different settings and situations. While this involves skill teaching, a meaningful accountability system and approach, and consistency, it also requires you to use the "if your consequate, you must educate" principle when dealing with students who still make Bad Choices.

The Importance of Consistency

As noted throughout this manual, effective teaching requires the use of skills, accountability, and consistency. This reading begins with a summary of the important points that have been emphasized regarding consistency.

Consistency and Teaching Social Skills

- The effective teaching of prosocial skills requires that you teach those skills consistently and that you consistently apply classroom- and building-based incentives and consequences. That is, you need to teach, model, and reinforce the Stop & Think process in the same way over time and across different circumstances. You also need to follow through with incentives and consequences for Good and Bad Choices, respectively, at least 80% of the time.

- If you do not consistently follow through with incentives and consequences when you use them to motivate students' Good Choices, you will potentially reinforce students' inappropriate behavior and undermine your accountability system.

- You also need to be consistent across the individual students in your classrooms. If you are inconsistent across students, individual students may decide that your incentive and consequence system is confusing (at best) or unfair (at worst).

- In addition, you need to recognize that students have their own "histories of inconsistency" and that these histories influence how long you need to be consistent when implementing new interventions or programs designed to improve student behavior. Indeed, you need to implement and maintain new behavioral interventions beyond a student's history of past (intervention) inconsistency.

- In the absence of consistency, students learn to distrust the rules, how those rules are applied, and who applies them. As inconsistency increases, students become unmotivated and unresponsive, and their behavior becomes random or disorganized because they do not know what is expected of them.

- The impact of inconsistency on students' behavior can be reversed. The longer a student has experienced inconsistency, however, the longer the adults in that student's life need to maintain a consistent behavioral environment in order to have a positive and long-lasting behavioral impact on the student.

To summarize, you need to teach the Stop & Think process consistently, use the Stop & Think language consistently, and use and reinforce Stop & Think skills at school and in other settings consistently over time. You also need to be consistent, at appropriate developmental and maturational levels, with the Stop & Think process from student to student. Students want their lives to be structured and predictable, and they want to know that adults' expectations for their behavior will be dependable and fair. Even though they are sometimes resistant, students want to know what the Good Choices and Bad Choices are for specific situations, and they want incentives and consequences to be applied logically, equitably, and consistently.

How Inconsistency Strengthens Inappropriate Behavior

The most important concept to grasp regarding consistency and inconsistency is how inconsistency strengthens inappropriate or Bad Choice behavior. There are three primary ways that this occurs in many classrooms.

1. Teachers often (appropriately) tell their students what they need to do to make a Good Choice, but then they often (inappropriately) don't follow through to ensure that the Good Choice is made, or they don't follow through quickly enough such that the Good Choice is made well after the teacher wants it to be made.

2. Teachers often (appropriately) tell their students what will happen if they make a Bad Choice but then (inappropriately) don't follow through with the consequences when a student makes a Bad Choice. Instead, the teacher accepts the inappropriate behavior and then often delivers a new ultimatum, giving the student yet another chance when he or she should have made the Good Choice the first time.

3. Teachers often (appropriately) tell their students what will happen if they make a Bad Choice, deliver the consequence (appropriately) when a student actually makes a Bad Choice, but then (inappropriately) do not do the same thing the next time.

The following sections take a closer look at each of these three scenarios.

"This Is the Last Time I'll Tell You to Quiet Down and Complete Your Seatwork"

Over the course of a typical day, many teachers ask their students to quiet down and complete some task. The important questions you need to ask yourself are: "How quickly do my students quiet down and begin their work?" "How many times do they have to be reminded?" "Has a pattern developed where students don't respond until I have given a certain number of reminders?" When such a pattern exists, the inappropriate behavior is the students' decision to not quiet down when asked the first time and/or to not quiet down within a reasonable amount of time. However, it is likely that the teacher's inconsistency has created the problem.

Consider a common situation such as: asking your students to quiet down and complete a task. What do you do when they do not comply within your expected amount of time? If you follow the noncompliance with a Stop & Think cue, telling your students that they need to follow your direction within a specified period of time and then telling them what will happen after they make a Good Choice or a Bad Choice, respectively, then you are doing a good job. But this is only true if you follow through with the incentives or consequences immediately after they make the Good or Bad Choice. An even better job would be for you to define your behavioral expectations and the possible incentives and consequences right from the beginning when you first assign the task.

If you ask the students to quiet down and complete a task and then go back to your desk, allowing your students to continue talking and to ignore your request, then you, like your students, are making a Bad Choice. Moreover, if you return ten or 15 minutes later, get angry at the students, tell them again to get to work on the task, and then disappear again to your desk without making sure that the students comply, then you have compounded your Bad Choice.

Finally, if you return five minutes later, get angry at the students again, and then guide them through your request—ensuring this time that they comply—then you have taught your students that they must be accountable to you only after your third request, only after you get "really angry," and only when you actually guide them toward complete compliance. Your inconsistency in not holding your students immediately accountable to your request or direction results in a behavioral pattern where they don't independently make the Good Choice and they wait for you to manage their behavior.

The solution to this situation is to (1) teach the **Following Directions** skill, (2) link your **Following Directions** requests to meaningful incentives and consequences, and (3) be very consistent early on in following up with these incentives and consequences. Once your students have mastered the **Following Directions** skill—where mastery means responding to the direction the first time without complaints—they will more automatically respond to your directions the first time, and you will not always have to "force" them to comply. Once this is accomplished, you will need to consistently reinforce your students' Good Choices, but you will not have to consistently manage their behavior.

"Go Ahead . . . Step Over That Line"

The second type of teacher inconsistency occurs when teachers identify consequences for when their students make Bad Choices and then do not follow through when the Bad Choices are made. Here, teachers have figuratively drawn a line in the sand, telling their students not to cross it. But when a student actually steps across the line, the teachers do not consequate the inappropriate behavior. Instead, they redraw the line (often with a different behavioral expectation) and then identify a new contingency or consequence (which often is more intense or restrictive than the previous one). Thus, the students learn that they can successfully ignore, delay, or avoid the first expectation and then get a second chance to follow their teachers' directions. They ultimately learn that their teachers really do not mean what they say (the first, second, or third time) when they link certain Bad Choice behaviors to certain consequences. These Bad Choice behaviors often become more frequent, longer, or more intense when this pattern of inconsistency occurs.

This "step over that line" pattern can also occur in the opposite direction. For example, there are times when teachers ask their students to make Good Choices and then specify an incentive or reward that will be provided when the Good Choice is made. Then, after the students have made a Good Choice and done their part, the teachers do not provide the positive reinforcement promised or delay its delivery such that it is no longer linked with the original Good Choice. While these delays sometimes occur unintentionally, teachers must understand that students may become hesitant or distrustful of such promises in the future.

Ultimately, this pattern of inconsistency results in (1) students who are not motivated by their teachers' incentives or consequences; (2) students who ignore or do not trust their teachers to follow through with stated expectations, incentives, and consequences; (3) students whose inappropriate behavior or resistance to their teachers increases over time; (4) students who feel their teachers are being unfair when the teachers finally do deliver a consequence; and/or (5) teachers who must use a more intense consequence in order to get their students' attention and compliance.

"But I'm Tired . . ."

The third way that teachers strengthen students' inappropriate behavior through inconsistency is when they tell their students what will happen if the students make a Bad Choice, appropriately deliver the consequence when a student actually makes the Bad Choice, but then do not consistently provide this consequence when the student does the same thing at another time. This is the "but I'm tired" response.

Imagine that you have a student who often calls out answers, without raising his or her hand and waiting to be acknowledged, to get attention. To address this problem, you institute a classroom rule that any student who calls out an answer loses a point on your daily incentive and reinforcement system. On the day that you first implement this rule, your student quickly calls out an answer and you quickly deduct a point from his or her chart. Later on that day, the same thing happens while the class is working in cooperative groups, but you decide that you are too tired (or too busy or too annoyed or too something) to walk over and deduct a point from the student's chart.

So, what happens because of your inconsistency? Typically, the result will be an increase in the student's calling out because (1) the student interprets your decision to not deduct a point as a message that some calling out is okay, (2) the student wants to see how many call-outs he can "get away with" before you finally consequate his behavior, or (3) the student assumes that your first response (when you did deduct a point on his chart) was random and will be inconsistent in the future.

Students' behavior can be very challenging and tiresome at times. Nonetheless, if you become tired and do not maintain a high level of consistency when you link Good Choices with incentives and Bad Choices with consequences, then you will actually need to spend more time relinking these choices and responses in the future. Thus, when you begin to consistently respond to your students with appropriate incentives and consequences for specific situations, you must maintain this pattern until the students' behavior is more automatic and they master the applicable skill.

The good news, however, is that you should not have to maintain 100% consistency with your students for specific behaviors forever. Over time—and often very quickly if you always start from a position of consistency—you can decrease the need for high levels of consistency. At this point, your students are typically managing their own behavior, and instead of focusing on consequences, you can begin to positively reinforce their appropriate behavior (e.g., students' ability to play a game together appropriately, students supporting and reinforcing one another, and students showing good sportsmanship). However, if you decrease your consistency too quickly—or become inconsistent altogether—you will undermine your hard work and increase your students' Bad Choices.

A Note About Punishment and Identifying the "Can't Do" Versus "Won't Do" Child

It cannot be stressed enough that consequences are not the same as punishments. Consequences are meant to motivate students to make Good Choices as they focus on avoiding Bad Choices and the consequences for them. Punishment is meant to chastise or penalize inappropriate behavior that has just occurred with the hope of stopping it from happening in the future.

The reason it is necessary to distinguish between consequences and punishment is that behavior is changed through teaching, not punishment. And while consequences can be a valuable part of the teaching process (remember: "If you consequate, you must educate"), punishment is not a teaching process at all. The Stop & Think social skills process is completely based on the need to teach prosocial behaviors when they do not exist and to teach replacement behaviors when inappropriate behaviors already exist. In this context, consequences can be an effective component of this teaching process.

A number of very important principles exist regarding punishment, some of which may challenge what you now believe.

Punishment and Performance-Deficit Students vs. Skill-Deficit Students

As noted earlier, punishment doesn't change behavior, education changes behavior. For many years, educators believed that punishment changed behavior. After all, when they punished a student, often the student would later conform or would respond appropriately the next time. However, when this change in behavior occurred, if it occurred at all, it was typically because the student already had the skills or ability to perform the desired behavior, he or she had simply been choosing not to use the skills. This is the definition of a student with a performance deficit.

Remember that a student with a performance deficit has already learned a desired skill (e.g., following directions, sharing, verbalizing anger in words and not actions), but he or she does not demonstrate the skill. Often, the skill is not demonstrated because (1) the student chooses not to perform the appropriate behavior, (2) the student has not received enough intrinsic or extrinsic incentive to perform the behavior, (3) the student has not received adult permission to perform the behavior or a prompt indicating that the behavior is needed, or (4) the student does not realize that the behavior is appropriate at the time or in the situation. The last two reasons involve problems of generalization. That is, while the student may have mastered a specific behavior in one setting, for one social situation, or with certain people, he or she has not learned that the same behavior is needed or would be useful in other settings or situations or with different people.

Performance deficits need to be contrasted with skill deficits. A skill deficit occurs when a student has not learned a specific social skill or has not learned that skill to mastery. If a student has not learned certain skills, the most direct intervention is teaching. For example, if a student does not know how to log on to a computer properly and has never been taught how to do so, then a teacher needs to teach the skill through instruction, modeling, role playing, and performance feedback until it is mastered. Similarly, if a student has never learned how to ignore a peer's distractions, then a teacher needs to teach this skill, provide practice opportunities, and reinforce the skill before expecting the student to demonstrate it independently.

The second part of the skill-deficit definition requires an understanding of mastery. Mastery involves teaching students so well that they can perform a skill automatically, almost without thinking, and under conditions of stress or emotionality (e.g., anger, fear, anxiety, lack of self-confidence). Mastery also involves some aspects of generalization or the transfer of training. That is, students need to be taught to successfully transfer and correctly use their skills across time, settings, people, situations, and different levels of emotion. This part of the definition is very important, because some students can perform a skill successfully when things are calm or when in certain settings, but they are unable to perform the same skill successfully when under stress or in different settings.

To summarize, performance-deficit students are students who "won't do" what they are asked; skill-deficit students are those who "can't do" what they are asked. You need to be able to distinguish between "can't do" and "won't do" students and situations. Given the definition of mastery and the stresses that students continuously experience in their lives, it is likely that most students will be "can't do" students until they have sufficient learning and opportunities to practice their prosocial skills. Thus, it is important that you remember you are a teacher first and a disciplinarian second. Finally, if you are ever unsure of whether you have a "can't do" or a "won't do" student, assume that the student can't do the skill required and then proceed to teach the skill to mastery.

Punishment and Anger

Punishment—especially when it involves force and anger—only models force and anger. If teachers show students that problems are solved through the use of force or demonstrations of power, then students will learn to use the same approaches when they have to do their own problem solving. Clearly, anger and force are incompatible with the social skills process that students need to learn and practice. Punishment is not an effective interpersonal, problem-solving, or conflict resolution skill. At best, punishment will confuse a student who is learning the Stop & Think social skills process. At worst, punishment will undermine the process, making it ineffective.

It is important to note that when punishment is used with a "can't do" student, it may result in a related kind of anger. If a student is being punished for not performing a behavior or completing a task that he or she is truly unable to perform or complete, he or she may become frustrated and angry because the punishment cannot be avoided and is unfair. While the student might become withdrawn or depressed, as in learned helplessness, the anger response is more likely, given the modeling effect described previously.

Punishment and Avoiding Responsibility

When schools use corporal punishment as well as consequences (approximately 20 states still allow corporal punishment), some students learn that it is easier and takes less time to receive a punishment (e.g., a spanking) than to have to "repay" a Bad Choice through a consequence (e.g., an apology and an effort to repair or remediate the situation). When this occurs, these students will begin to choose punishments over consequences in the future. Clearly, the use of corporal punishment undermines the teaching, practicing, and reinforcing of prosocial choices and behaviors. Further, it allows these students to escape from being accountable for their Good and Bad Choices and from needing to take responsibility for their actions. Finally, it reinforces the "quick-fix" perspective of some students that allows them to avoid the practice needed to learn self-management and independent thinking and behavioral skills.

Appendix C: Glossary

Accountability — A system or individual interactions that motivate students toward Good Choices and away from Bad Choices, respectively. Meaningful incentives and consequences are the key as students make Good Choices either because they are motivated by the incentives they will receive for Good Choices or by the consequences they will receive if they make Bad Choices.

Building-Level School Climate or School Discipline and Safety Team — A team whose members represent the various constituencies of a building who monitor the classroom implementation of the *Stop & Think Social Skills Program*; the building's accountability and consistency system; the training needs and implementation process for the staff; the progress and success of the discipline and behavior management program; and the more pervasive safety and security needs of the students, staff, and building. While the grade-level social skills team leaders form the core of this team, other School Climate team members typically include the building principal; teachers from special education and curricular support (i.e., Title I, reading/math support); teachers from special arts or enrichment teachers (i.e., music, art, P.E., media); pupil personnel specialists (i.e., school psychologist, social worker, and/or counselor educators); classroom paraprofessionals or teacher assistants; and support personnel (i.e., secretarial, cafeteria, custodial, and/or bus drivers).

Choice Skills — Social skills whose skill scripts reflect a number of possible Good Choices that students can make in order to successfully demonstrate the skill. For example, in order to deal with teasing, students have a number of Good Choices available as part of the skill script, such as ignore, ask the person to stop, walk away, or find an adult for help.

Conflict — Situations where student disagreements or power struggles occur, either overtly or covertly. Conflicts occur either externally or internally. That is, they originate either because of *external* people, events, or situations or because of *internal* perceptions, beliefs, self-statements, or expectations.

Conflict Resolution Skills — Social skills that help students deal with significant emotions and emotional situations and resolve existing intrapersonal and interpersonal conflicts. Examples of conflict resolution social skills are: Dealing With Teasing, Dealing With Losing, Dealing With Anger, Walking Away From a Fight, Dealing With Accusations, Dealing With Being Left Out, Dealing With Peer Pressure, Dealing With Fear, and Dealing With Another Person's Anger.

Consequences—Actions or responses that occur after or in anticipation of students' Bad Choices that motivate them to make a Good Choice the next time. In general, the mildest possible consequence needed to motivate a student's Good Choice should be used. As consequences get more negative or intense, some students need at least the same level of intensity in order for the consequences to maintain their meaningfulness over time.

Consistency—More of a process than something that teachers explicitly teach (as in skills) or provide (as in incentives and consequences). Initially, consistency involves teachers' consistent teaching of the Stop & Think social skills and their consistent use of classroom- and building-based incentives and consequences. More broadly, consistency involves all of the teachers, staff, and students in a school as they implement social skills and accountability processes in the same way across time, settings, situations, and circumstances.

Cues—The physiological reactions that indicate how a student is emotionally responding to a situation that either can facilitate or interfere with problem resolution.

Effective Classroom Teacher/Staff Development Component—One of Project ACHIEVE's Implementation Components that focuses on ensuring that effective instructional styles and teaching behaviors are used in the classroom with students along with appropriate curricular procedures and materials. In doing this, the goal is to maximize students' attention to task, academic engaged time, academic learning time, and their specific and general achievement.

Five-to-One Rule—The rule that states that students need to be in classroom environments that provide five positive interactions for every negative interaction. To follow this rule, teachers need to recognize that there are at least three sources of positive or negative interactions in any environment: the adults, other students or peers, and the students themselves. Thus, teachers need to (1) provide as many positive interactions with their students as they can, (2) teach and reinforce all of the students in their classrooms and around their schools to be positive to each other, and (3) teach their students to self-reinforce and become positive advocates for themselves.

Grade-Level Social Skills Team Leaders—Individual teachers chosen at each grade or cluster level who help oversee the social skills process in a building by guiding and monitoring the implementation of the social skills process within their grade levels while linking the grade level to the entire building relative to social skills implementation and student discipline and behavior.

Histories of Inconsistency—The amount of past inconsistency relative to social skills, interventions, and/or accountability that a student has experienced. Teachers, need to functionally identify students' individual histories of inconsistency recognizing that these histories influence how long they (the teachers) need to be consistent when implementing new interventions or programs designed to improve student behavior. Ultimately, teachers need to implement new interventions past a student's history of past inconsistency.

"If You Consequate, You Must Educate" Rule—The rule that states that if a student needs to receive a consequence for inappropriate behavior, the consequence should be followed up with three positive practice opportunities as soon as reasonably possible.

Incentives—Actions or responses that occur after or in anticipation of students' Good Choices that motivate their behavior or continuing behavior. Incentives are either extrinsic (e.g., involving tangible or overt reinforcers) or intrinsic (e.g., involving positive self-statements like "Tell yourself you did a Great Job!" or "Give yourself a big pat on the back for making such a Good Choice!").

Instructional Consultation and Curriculum-Based Assessment Component—One of Project ACHIEVE's Implementation Components that focuses on the belief that the learner is part of an instructional system that involves interdependent interactions between task demands (i.e., what needs to be learned?), the instruction (i.e., are appropriate instructional and management strategies available and being used?), and the student (i.e., is the student ready and capable of learning?). This component focuses on the functional, curriculum-based assessment of referred students' learning problems by evaluating their progress in and response to the curriculum, their ability to succeed in the curriculum, and the instructional processes needed to teach them to skill mastery.

Interpersonal Skills—Social skills that help students to interact appropriately with siblings, peers, older and younger students, parents, teachers, and other adults such that they "get along with each other." These are the skills that help us to build and maintain social relationships. Examples of interpersonal social skills are Sharing, Asking for Permission, Joining an Activity, Contributing to Discussions/Answering Classroom Questions, How to Interrupt, How to Wait for Your Turn, How to Wait for an Adult's Attention, Beginning/Ending a Conversation, Giving/Accepting a Compliment.

Logical Consequences—Consequences that occur after a student has made a Bad Choice and that are logically tied or related to the situation and the inappropriate behavior. Examples of logical consequences might be: (1) you tell a student you cannot talk or respond to him or her for a short period of time even after the "waiting" time is over, (2) you withhold the incentive that was promised, and (3) you have your students practice the Waiting for Your Turn skill an extra three minutes after not performing the skill successfully.

Modeling—Modeling occurs during a social skills lesson when a teacher demonstrates a new social skill by acting out a situation related to the social skill and verbalizing the skill script. Here, teachers need to clearly verbalize the Stop & Think steps while showing their students how to perform the appropriate behavior. In other words, during the teaching process, teachers need to both show and tell their students how to perform a desired behavior.

Natural Consequences—Consequences that occur after a student has made a Bad Choice and that occur normally or naturally as a result of the inappropriate behavior. Examples here might include the class period going longer than expected and your students missing a special activity or opportunity that was promised for appropriate behavior, or your continued refusal to attend to a student while he or she is not waiting appropriately for his or her turn.

Parent Training, Tutoring, and Support Component—One of Project ACHIEVE's Implementation Components that focuses on increasing the involvement of all parents in all facets of the program, but especially the involvement of parents of at-risk, underachieving, and special education students. This component focuses on the development of ongoing home-school collaboration by (1) making parents an integral part of the planning and activities of the school, (2) helping parents to understand teachers' expectations of their children and to increase their support of their children's academic and social development, (3) increasing parent-to-parent communication and resource building, and (4) supporting parent-to-teacher collaboration so as to build effective home-school partnerships.

Performance Deficits—This occurs when a student has mastered a specific social skill but chooses not to demonstrate it. Performance-deficit students are students who won't do what they are asked; skill-deficit students are those who can't do what they are asked.

Performance Feedback—The feedback that teachers give during a social skills lesson while students are practicing a new social skill using role playing. This feedback should positively reinforce the students as they correctly (1) verbalize the social skills script, (2) demonstrate the appropriate skill or behavior, and (3) review their performance after the role play or practice session is over. If a student incorrectly verbalizes a social skill script or practices the wrong steps, the teacher's feedback should describe what he or she needs to do to correct the situation. After this description, the student should practice the social skill and the skill script again, making sure that the correct script is used and the appropriate behaviors are demonstrated.

Physical or Self-Awareness—Students' awareness of the physical and emotional reactions or cues that occur in different situations (both positive and negative). When difficult situations occur, this awareness may include what students say inside their heads, how they emotionally feel, the ways that their bodies react internally. When awareness exist, students know that these physiological reactions are occurring before they behaviorally respond. These reactions cue students that they are responding to a situation and may need to use the Stop & Think process to make a Good Choice.

Positive Practice Opportunities—Times when a student is made to practice a prosocial skill immediately after making a Bad Choice. The prosocial skill is the behavior that the student should have demonstrated; thus, it is directly related (and "opposite") to the Bad Choice behavior. Teachers are encouraged to provide students with two to three positive practice opportunities as soon as possible after their Bad Choices (and consequences) when things have calmed down. Positive practice opportunities increase the probability that students will make a Good Choice the next time.

Problem-Solving Skills—Social skills that help students to solve individual, interactive, or group (e.g., peer or family) problems. Some of these skills are important as they prevent problems from occurring, while others of these skills are important because they help students to respond to a problem so that it does not escalate into a conflict. Examples of problem-solving social skills are: Asking for Help, Apologizing, Accepting Consequences, Setting a Goal, Deciding What to Do, Avoiding Trouble, Understanding Your/Others' Feelings, and Responding to Failure.

Project ACHIEVE—A school-based/whole-school professional development program that teaches and reinforces critical staff skills and intervention approaches that focus on helping building staff to strategically plan for and address the immediate and long-term academic and behavioral needs of all students. Project ACHIEVE places particular emphasis on increasing student performance in the areas of social skills and conflict resolution, improving student achievement and academic progress, facilitating positive school climates, and in increasing parental involvement and support. This is done through an integrated process that involves organizational and resource development, comprehensive inservice training and follow-up, and parent and community involvement which all lead to direct and preventive services for our at-risk students.

Project ACHIEVE's Four Implementation Models—(1) The Strategic Planning model, (2) The Organizational and Integrated Services model, (3) The Problem-Solving and Student Learning and Instruction model, and (4) The School Safety and Effective Behavior Management model.

Project ACHIEVE's Implementation Components—(1) Strategic Planning and Organizational Analysis and Development; (2) Referral Question Consultation Process (RQC); (3) Effective Classroom Teaching/Staff Development; (4) Instructional Consultation and Curriculum-Based Assessment; (5) Behavioral Consultation and Behavioral Interventions, including the schoolwide and parent/community use of social skills (or problem solving) and aggression control training; (6) Parent Training, Tutoring, and Support; and (7) Research and Accountability.

Punishment—An act, typically of retribution, that occurs to respond to students' already exhibited Bad Choices. Punishment also occurs in an attempt to stop a student from making the same Bad Choice in the future without regard for what prosocial skill the student needs to demonstrate instead. Thus, while the student may not make the same Bad Choice, there is no assurance that he or she will make a Good Choice. Finally, punishment generally models negatively and retribution as a mode of teaching and problem solving.

Referral Question Consultation Process (RQC) Component—One of Project ACHIEVE's Implementation Components that is grounded in the belief that school systems and building staff must utilize a common language and method of problem solving in order to address potential or referred problems. RQC training facilitates a conceptual shift in the service-delivery philosophy of the building from a refer-test-place approach to one of problem solving, consultation, and classroom-based intervention.

Research and Accountability Component—One of Project ACHIEVE's Implementation Components that focuses on an active research program investigating critical consultation and/or curricular and behavioral intervention variables and techniques within Project ACHIEVE. This component also provides ongoing feedback as to the time- and cost-effectiveness of Project ACHIEVE. Finally, it provides formative evaluation feedback such that the project can be adapted at the building level with greater effectiveness and accountability.

Role Play—Role playing occurs during a social skills lesson when a student (or students) is chosen to practice a new social skill by acting out a situation related to the social skill and verbalizing the skill script. Here, the student needs to clearly verbalize the Stop & Think steps while demonstrating how to perform the prosocial behavior.

Self-Awareness or Physical Awareness—Students' awareness of the physical and emotional reactions or cues that occur in different situations (both positive and negative). When difficult situations occur, this awareness may include what students say inside their heads, how they emotionally feel, the ways that their bodies react internally. When awareness exist, students know that these physiological reactions are occurring before they behaviorally respond. These reactions cue students that they are responding to a situation and may need to use the Stop & Think process to make a Good Choice.

Self-Management—The integrated skills of self-awareness, self-control, self-instruction, self-monitoring, self-correction, and self-reinforcement.

Situational Awareness—Students' awareness of the situations (the people, places, times, activities, and other circumstances) that create certain emotional reactions or responses (positive and negative) and that might cause the most difficulty for them.

Skill Deficits—These occur when a student has not learned a specific social skill or has not learned that skill to mastery. The first part of this definition simply says that some students have not learned certain skills and that the most direct intervention for this is teaching. The second part of this definition reinforces the definition of skill mastery.

Social Skills—Positive or prosocial survival, interpersonal, problem-solving, and conflict resolution behaviors that students can learn so that they can interact with people and situations in appropriate ways.

Social Skills Application Activities—Once a teacher has taught a new social skill for the first three days, the social skills "lessons" for Thursday, Friday, and the next Monday (or, perhaps, including Tuesday) involve a 15- to 25-minute period, which normally occurs during the academic day, where the teacher integrates the social skill into the academic lesson. While this integration may be somewhat artificial, these application activities give students opportunities to practice the social skill in a more realistic way—in the context of the daily classroom routine. Over time, this process not only gives students more chances to practice the social skill and the skill script, but it also helps the students to transfer their social skill training into real settings and situations.

Social Skills, Behavioral Consultation, and Behavioral Interventions Component—One of Project ACHIEVE's Implementation Components that focuses on the analysis and implementation of effective behavioral interventions that are designed to resolve students' curricular and behavioral problems or to improve teachers' instructional and classroom management procedures.

Social Skills Infusion Activities—During the last three or four days of the two-week social skills teaching cycle, teachers infuse social skills practice and reinforcement whenever possible. Here, they prompt and reinforce students at every reasonable opportunity for using the social skill and the script that has been taught and reinforced during the past week and a half. Here, teachers are looking for "teachable moments" when the social skill can be naturally practiced and/or reinforced.

Social Skills Master Calendar—A calendar, received by all building staff, that outlines a recommended sequence of social skills, each skill's recommended teaching steps, and a suggested schedule for the week when each skill will be taught (either buildingwide or at a specific grade level).

Social Skills Mastery—Mastery occurs when students successfully or positively demonstrate an academic skill or interpersonal (social skill) under all conditions, including under conditions of emotionality.

Social Skills Script—The verbalization of the Stop & Think steps with the specific steps or choices of the chosen social skill (e.g., Listening, Following Directions). Just like an actor's script, the verbal script tells a student, step by step, how to perform a specific social skill. The script is the key to the entire Stop & Think teaching process.

Social Skills Teaching—The formal classroom lesson that begins the formal teaching process for any social skill, which typically occurs on Monday, Tuesday, and Wednesday of the first week. It involves a 25- to 30-minute social skill class where teachers teach the social skill, model it, and provide numerous opportunities for students to role play the social skill and script. For kindergarten and first grade, this teaching likely occurs during their "circle time" in the morning and may not take the full 25 minutes. These teachers need to adapt the teaching process to take into account their students' developmental levels and needs (probably using puppets or other adaptations for the role plays and visuals instead of writing for the skill steps). For grades 2–6, social skills lessons are taught between the first and second academic periods of the morning.

Social Skills Two-Week Teaching Schedule—The recommended two-week schedule used to teach a new social skill. This schedule involves three days of skill teaching, three to four days of skill application, and three to four days of skill infusion, all occurring in the classroom setting directed by the classroom teacher.

Sound Bites—Collapsing the Stop & Think steps or choices for a particular social skill into short words or phrases that can cue the appropriate behavior without having to go through all of the script or language. Sound bites facilitate the memorization of the social skill steps and the process that results in students automatically demonstrating a skill without needing to go through the script at all.

Special Situations—Buildingwide behavioral situations involving problems that occur in a school's more public areas and that involve students but are not completely caused by or solved through interventions only with these students. Often, special situations involve problems in such places as the school's cafeteria, hallways, buses, recess or playgrounds, or media centers or other common areas.

Step Skills—Social skills whose skill scripts reflect a specific sequence of steps that students must perform in order to successfully demonstrate the skill. For example, in order to Follow Directions, students need to listen to the direction, understand the direction, decide what the response to the direction requires, and prepare to follow the direction.

Step and Choice Skills—Social skills whose skill scripts reflect a number of possible good choices that are embedded in a specific sequence. Both the skill steps and the choices within these steps must be performed in order for students to successfully demonstrate the skill. For example, in order to deal with anger, students need to first "take a deep breath and count to five"; then they think about their possible Good Choices (e.g., tell the person they are angry, walk away for now, ask an adult for help); then they need to choose the best choice from those taught or generated.

Stop & Think Social Skills Steps—The five steps that are used to teach, implement, and reinforce every social skill: (1) Stop and Think! (2) Are you going to make a Good Choice or Bad Choice? (3) What are your Choices or Steps? (4) Do It! (5) Good Job!

Stop & Think Teaching Process—The teaching process that is used when teaching every social skill: teaching the steps of the desired social skill; modeling the steps and the social skills language (or script); role playing the steps and the script with students; providing performance feedback to students relative to how accurately they are verbalizing the skill script and how successfully they are behaviorally demonstrating the new skill; and applying the skill and its steps as much as possible during the day to reinforce the teaching over time, in different settings, with different people, and in different situations.

Strategic Planning and Organizational Analysis and Development Component—One of Project ACHIEVE's Implementation Components that initially focuses on assessing the organizational climate, administrative style, staff decision making, and other interactive processes at a Project ACHIEVE school. It moves eventually, and as needed, into the development of new organizational patterns and interactions that facilitate and support the academic and social progress of the school's student body.

Survival Skills—Social skills that are prerequisite and used, directly or indirectly, by all of the other social skills in order for them to be performed successfully. These skills form the foundation for all other skills, and typically, many of them are taught first as students are growing up. Examples of survival social skills are: Listening, Following Directions, Ignoring Distractions, Using Nice Talk, Using Brave Talk, Rewarding Yourself, Evaluating Yourself.

Teachable Moments—A naturally-occurring moment in a classroom or other setting when a social skill can be prompted, retaught, or reinforced. There are three types of teachable moments. They occur (1) when students have successfully demonstrated an appropriate social skill, and teachers can reinforce the verbal script that they must have used to attain this success; (2) when students have made a Bad Choice, demonstrating an inappropriate social skill, leaving the teacher with the opportunity to have them use the correct skill and verbal script ideally to remediate the situation; and (3) when students are faced with a problem or situation that can be solved by choosing and using the appropriate social skill and script.

Transfer of Training—After a social skill initially has been taught, the act of transferring the training from the teaching situation to everyday use. Here, teachers use the social skills that have been taught as much as possible from day to day, hour to hour, and minute to minute so that students begin to use the skill independently across time, settings, people, situations, and circumstances.

Triggers—Actual situations in the classroom, around the school, and with the peer group that cause or create a "social skills dilemma" whereby students need to decide if they are going to make a Good Choice or a Bad Choice.

Ordering Information

The *Stop & Think Social Skills Program* is available for Grades PreK-1, Grades 2-3, Grades 4-5, and Grades 6-8

Classroom Sets at each level include:

- Teacher's Manual
- Reproducible Signs and Forms
- Skill Cards for Students
- Posters and Stickers

For information and pricing on these products, or for information on training for the *Stop & Think Social Skills Program*, call **1-800-547-6747**, or visit our website at **www.sopriswest.com**